The Little Book of
SLANG
SAYINGS, JARGON
& HUMOUR

DEDICATION

....

To all friends, family and former colleagues who made
this book possible with their valuable contributions.
To George, Gladys and Costas – the parents who are
no longer with us but whose memory lives on.

The Little Book of
SLANG
SAYINGS, JARGON
& HUMOUR

Michael Layton QPM
Androulla Christou-Layton

BREWIN BOOKS

BREWIN BOOKS
19 Enfield Ind. Estate,
Redditch,
Worcestershire,
B97 6BY
www.brewinbooks.com

Published by Brewin Books 2021

A CIP catalogue record for this book is
available from the British Library.

ISBN: 978-1-85858-735-6

Printed and bound in Great Britain
by Severn, Gloucester

CONTENTS

INTRODUCTION

The use of sayings, abbreviations and slang is not unique to one culture, race, faith, place or profession. Some of the words or phrases listed in this book have a serious intent and others are designed to be humorous or light-hearted. Most have evolved over time and some are enshrined in history.

This little book is not designed to be an academic study of the origins of these phrases nor indeed a comprehensive dictionary in its own right, rather it has been created to provide some light-hearted reading and hopefully to rekindle some positive memories of past experiences in life.

We should not seek to judge the merits or otherwise of some of these sayings by the standards and expectations of today's society. We learn from our history which provides the template from which others will learn to create their own history and to determine their own ethics and standards appropriate to that period.

From our experience classifying phrases and sayings into specific categories or based on geographical locations always creates a forum for debate as to who 'owns' their origins. This becomes no more evident than when it comes to who 'owns' Birmingham and Black Country sayings, with vigorous debates and strong views on both sides of the argument.

Our answer is that in many cases we simply don't know but what we do know is that as people migrate to different places, for example for employment or a change in family circumstances, they take their language with them and it should therefore be no surprise that the same, or similar, phrases will be used in more than one location. We leave that debate to the experts!

Clearly in more recent decades as transport and communication links have improved the potential for greater population movements have increased still further.

Some may ask how the specific categories were arrived at in this book and the answer is relatively simple – for the most part they represent places, people, friends, family past and present, and colleagues that we know and therefore feel connected to. Many of them participated in providing material and had some fun along the way in doing so, whilst reminding us of the richness of the diverse nature of our connections.

The categories are as such in many ways a personal reflection of who we are and our life experiences and, in that context, if another family were writing this book, we would expect the categories to be somewhat different.

Language is an important part of our sense of identity and variations in terms of slang and sayings provide a unique insight into how we communicate with each other at different levels. In the UK alone it is estimated that there are at least fifty-six regional accents.

As a born and bred 'Brummie' I have over the years learned to live with the 'pain' of people who have tried and usually failed to 'mimic' the voice of Jasper Carrott in a poor attempt at recreating a Birmingham accent. We 'are what we are' and thus I remain hugely proud of my ability to 'talk through my nose!'

The challenges are the same the world over as communities grapple with local variations, for example my wife and co-author Andry originates from Cyprus and speaks Greek with a blend of local dialects.

Above all else we don't want you to take this book too seriously and hope that you just simply enjoy the read – if the book brings but one smile to the readers face, we will have succeeded in our aim.

Michael Layton

1

MY MUM'S SAYINGS

'Ask your Dad' – avoiding the question.

'Back in my day' – memories of bygone days.

'Because I said so' – not negotiable.

'Button it' – be quiet.

'Charlie's Dead' – petticoat showing below the hem of a skirt.

'Chin Wag' – have a good chat.

'Do as I say – not as I do' – this is not a democracy.

'Don't try and teach Granny to suck eggs' – don't try to give advice to someone in relation to a subject that they already know more about than you.

'Down the Lane' – a reference to shopping with the co-author's parents in Ladypool Road, Sparkbrook on a Saturday in the 1960s.

'Eat your crusts – you'll get curly hair' – *'waste not want not'* – don't leave food on your plate.

'Fibbing' – telling untruths.

'Frock' – dress.

'Get your skates on' – hurry up.

'Glad Rags' – best clothes.

'His bit on the side' – mistress to a married man.

'If someone asked you to jump off a cliff would you do it' – highlighting stupidity.

'It's like Blackpool illuminations in here' – a reference to wasting electricity with all the lights on in the house.

'It will all end in tears' – one way or another pain is going to be inflicted.

'I've told you a thousand times' – the answer will still be *'NO'*.

'I want, never gets' – making demands doesn't work.

'Move away from the TV – you will get square eyes' – stop standing in front of the TV.

'Nan' – grandmother.

'Nice as pie' – pleasant to someone.

'No pudding unless you eat your dinner' – the element of bribery to avoid wasting food.

'Oh, I can't spit' – I'm thirsty.

'Oh, I'm spitting feathers' – a metaphor for having a dry mouth – usually when a cup of tea or *'cha'* is on *'the cards'* – in a different context can also mean being *'lost for words'* with anger.

'Pasty' – pale.

'Say pardon not what' – *'good manners maketh perfect'*.

'The proof of the pudding is in the eating' – the real value of something can only be judged from practical experience or results and not from appearance alone.

'There is no such word as can't' – compliance is inevitable.

'Tight fisted' – not *'free'* with their money' – like to hang onto it.

'Throw your teddy out of the pram' – behave in a bad-tempered manner.

'Umpteenth time' – referring to something that has happened many times before.

'Veg' – vegetables – as in *'meat and two veg'*.

'Wash your mouth out with soap' – the response to using a swear word.

'What did your last slave die of' – the lot of a housewife trying to do everything.

'What's for dinner Mum' – response – **'S**t with egg on'** – you'll get what's served and that's it.

'Who is she – the cat's mother?' – describing an *'old woman with grey whiskers'* – often used to reprimand children whenever they addressed adults in a disrespectful manner.

'Woke up with your backside in your hand' – grumpy, miserable, in a bad mood.

'You wait until your Dad gets home' – the threat of the slipper.

'You will take somebody's eye out with that' – dangerous play with various objects.

2

MY DAD'S SAYINGS

'A-A-A' – stop that immediately!

'About as useful as a fart in a cullender' – of no use at all.

'A load of old tat' – *'codswallop'* – *'cobblers'* – rubbish, nonsense.

'Ark at them' – listen to them.

'Barking Mad' – crazy or insane.

'Blow a fuse' – lose your temper.

'Bolt from the blue' – a complete surprise.

'Chuffed to bits' – happy.

'Come a Cropper' – fall heavily or suffer a defeat.

'Don't give a monkey's' – don't care – *'don't give a toss'*.

'Gobsmacked' – shocked – what happens when someone smacks you in the mouth.

'Gordon Bennett' – surprise and shock at the unexpected – like *'Cor Blimey'*.

'Half and half' – not one thing or another – a mixture.

'It's a load of old codswallop' – it's not worth the paper it's written on.

'I will give you a bunch of fives' – you will get a punch in the face.

'Kick in the teeth' – a blow or unpleasant setback – dates back to the 18th century.

'Kip' – sleep.

'Left hand doesn't know what the right hand is doing' – disorganised – in disarray.

'Money doesn't grow on trees' – *'not made of money'* – *'not loaded'* – applying caution as to how to spend money.

'Muggins' – an irreverent reference to oneself.

'No fool like an old fool' – an older person should know better than a younger person.

'Not even worth the tip' – useless rubbish.

'On the ropes' – struggling.

'On your bike' – *'get lost'* – go!

'Put a bit of elbow grease into it' – put a bit of effort into what you are doing.

'Put a sock in it' – shut up.

'Put your face straight' – stop looking miserable.

'Quacks' – the doctor.

'Rabbiting on' – talking a lot.

'Salt of the earth' – a good person.

'She's up the duff' – she's pregnant.

'Shut that door – were you born in a barn?' – trying to keep the house warm.

'Shut your Trap' – be quiet.

'Stick a broom up my arse' – expect me to do everything at the same time.

'Tatters' – collectors of scrap metal.

'There and back to see how far it is' – a deflection to a question as to where you were going.

'Too many fingers in the pie' – too many people getting involved or expressing an opinion – *'too many cooks spoil the broth'*.

'Until the cows come home' – for a very long time.

'Whiter than white' – beyond reproach.

'You have hit the nail on the head' – agreeing with what someone else is saying.

'You've made a right dog's dinner of that' – you've made a big mess.

'Zip it' – be quiet.

3

A BIT MORE 'BRUM' SLANG

Used by people living within the City of Birmingham
(Reference book *'Ta-Ra-A-Bit Our Kid'*
– available on Amazon.co.uk)

'A bit of a drip' – lacking in enthusiasm or energy.

'A face as long as Livery Street' – *'long face'* – miserable. A
reference to a long and straight street in Birmingham city-centre.

'A little bird told me' – a non-attributable comment.

'A moment on the lips is a lifetime on the hips' – a reference
to eating too many cream cakes.

'A trip down memory lane' – remembering the past.

'Babby' – baby or young child.

'Bags of' – lots of.

'Birmingham screwdriver' – hammer.

'Blowing your own trumpet' – *'bigging'* yourself up to others.

'Bluenose' – Birmingham City Football Club fan.

'Brew' – cup of tea.

'Brum' – Birmingham – *'Brummie'* – person from Birmingham.

'Buzz' – bus.

'Cag-handed' – clumsy.

'Chuffing' – eating.

'Coats and ats' – *'C & A'* clothing store in Birmingham city-centre.

'Cobbled together' – put together in a makeshift way.

'Def it' – forget it.

'Don't sit on top of the coal fire – you'll get corn beef legs' – you'll get burnt if you get too close to the fire.

'Down the Boozer' – at the pub – *'boozer'* a regular drinker.

'Drives us around the bend' – drives us mad or crazy.

'Ee-yar' – here you are.

'Fittle' – food.

'Garidge' – garage.

'Going around the Wrekin' – taking the long way around to get somewhere. The Wrekin is a hill in Shropshire.

'Heads should roll' – someone needs to pay the price for an alleged wrongdoing.

'I am as old as my gums but a bit older than my teeth' – (A phrase used by a Grandad from *'Brum'*).

'I'll meet you on the ramp' – a reference to the ramp leading up to the Birmingham Shopping Centre situated at the junction with New Street and Corporation Street.

'I'm off down the cut' – I'm off down the canal.

'It gave me the willies' – it scared me or gave me a fright.

'It's like New Street Station here' – crowded and busy – a reference to the central railway station in Birmingham.

'Lager Dash' – a pint of lager with a *'dash'* of lime juice in it.

'Lager Top' – a pint of lager with a *'dash'* of lemonade in it.

'Lamp someone' – hit them.

'Mutton dressed up as lamb' – an older woman dressed up to appear much younger but doesn't succeed.

'On my babbies life I'm telling the truth' – meant to stress that the individual was telling the truth. Often used during interviews with the police and rarely afforded much credence due to the ease with which the person was prepared to use it.

'Pat on the back' – congratulate.

'Pull the chain' – flush the toilet.

'Pull the wool over their eyes' – deceive them.

'Putting on airs and graces' – pretending to be *'posh'* – pretending to be someone that they were not – *'above one's station in life'*.

'Quit your belly-aching' – stop complaining.

'Red hat no drawers' – red hat – not wearing any underwear.

'Run around like a headless chicken' – *'Charge around like a bull in a china shop'* – a degree of panic, undiplomatic, not measured, controlled, or thoughtful of the consequences of their actions.

'Scrapping' – fighting.

'Second City' – Birmingham.

'Seeing what she's had for breakfast' – *'see next week's washing'* – an unexpected glimpse of a woman's underwear.

'Ta' – thanks.

'Tan yer arse' – give you a smack.

'Ta-Ra-A-Bit' Our Kid' – a familiar goodbye. Also, the title of one of the co-authored books on Birmingham slang with Stephen Burrows.

'The back of Rackhams' – a reference to *'ladies of the night'*. *'Rackhams'* is a well-known store in Birmingham city-centre but the location has no known connection to prostitution.

'Town' – Birmingham city-centre.

'Up the wooden hill' – go up to bed – *'up the wooden hill to Bedfordshire'*.

'Up to my eyeballs' – emphasizing the extreme degree of an undesirable situation – *'up to my neck'*.

'Well I'll go to the foot of our stairs' – an exclamation of surprise – originally from the North of England but in the 20th Century the phrase travelled to Birmingham.

'What do you call that – a cat's lick?' – the inability for someone, usually a child, to wash properly.

'Yam Yams' – a description by *'Brummies'* of people born in the Black Country.

'You've got a face like fourpence – put it straight' – a *'long face'* – miserable – change it.

* * *

A little bit of *'Brum'* fun from Janet Russell with very special thanks

"The trouble is if you put me in this book, you'll be thinking that I've *'got a bob on me self'*. There's all the usual like the *'miskins'*, and blokes *'going round the back'* when they went for a *'wee'* or *'going to turn their bike around'* for the same function. And some you don't hear now like *'bob howlers'* and a tall lad being *'Long Tom and a penny on the bottle'*, *'fossocking about'* and *'riling'* on chairs – which we seemed to do a lot as 'kids'. People don't seem to be as *'bandy as badgers'* now. There was a time when a lot of the *'old un's'* couldn't have stopped a *'pig in an entry'* bless em. And no-one goes a *'purler'* these days not even when given a right *'four'p'nee'un'*. To be honest you don't see people having a *'right up and a downer'* on the street on a Saturday night like you used to. A *'right straightener'* often used to put an end to long standing *'bull and cows'* between neighbours. I'm sure I can remember some of the old slang if I get my *'thinking cap'* on. I'm sure I saw some under the cushions on the *'squab'* in the *'glory hole'*...."

* * *

A little *'Brum'* slang poem with very special thanks to Lynn Selby who supports well-being through the use of poetry – email *lynn-selby@hotmail.co.uk*

~ Past Times ~

As we recollect our memories,

The language slips back too.

The dialect of the families

In cities and streets up and down.

It was black over Bill's Mother's

So said the sooted skies.

Mom would grab the washing

Pegs falling in her haste

The pinny round her waist, empty.

With a face as long as Livery Street,

She would herd us kids in

As thunder clapped her exit.

"Ark at that" shouted neighbour,

As she tried to beat the carpet.

"Floggin a dead horse" muttered Mom.

"That rug is as bare as my backside".

We giggled, but stopped short

As the kids on the bomb peck

Whistled and called us names.

"Play up yer own end" Mom bellowed.

Waving her Coronation tea towel

As they legged it to the Cut.

Tea was run round the table

But we never did rush,

Mom was daft as a brush, thinking

We would fall for that……. again.

Any road up, memories are soaked up now.

So up the dancers I go, happy with my past.

4

'BLACK COUNTRY' WEST MIDLANDS SLANG

Used by residents of Walsall, Wolverhampton,
Sandwell and Dudley in an industrial area
to the north and west of Birmingham.

'Agen' – again.

'Arr bay' – I'm not – *'Ay I'* – Am I not – *'Ay it'* – is it not.

'Arr bin yer arr kid ay'sin yow for ages' – how are you –
I haven't seen you for ages.

'Arr I am' – Yes, I am.

'Backerds' – backwards or back to front.

'Barmpot' – a silly person.

'Blartin' – crying – *'bawl'*.

'Bletter' – talk nonsense.

'Bost' – broken.

'Brummagem' – Birmingham.

'Chuck' – throw.

'Clobber' – clothes.

'Coot' – coat.

'Day' – didn't.

'Dow' – don't.

'Frit' – frightened.

'Gaffer' – employer – manager.

'Gawp' – stare.

'Gorra' – got.

'Gray Pays' – Grey Peas – traditional Black Country dish.

'Half-ender' – half a house brick.

'Have no cotter with' – have nothing to do with someone.

'Howm yeom doin' – how are you doing.

'I ay' – I'm not.

'I cor' – I can't.

'Jiffy' – moment.

'Kaylied' – drunk.

'Lughole' – ear.

'Lummocks' – a number of clumsy local people.

'Mate' – meat.

'Med' – made.

'Myther' – to become *'bothered'* – upset.

'Nanas' – bananas or silly people.

'Niggle' – find fault.

'Noggins' – a number of heads.

'Ommers' – hammers.

'Opple' – apple.

'Oss' – horse.

'Owamya' – how are you?

'Pop' – soft drink.

'Riffy' – dirty or unclean.

'Sadlers' – people who live in Walsall – links in with the history of leather and saddle making in the town.

'Scratchings' – a Black Country delicacy of deep-fried pork rind.

'Slummocking' – *'shuffling along'* – slowly, slovenly, slouching.

'Someat' – something.

'Sink' – basin.

'Spake' – speak.

'Suck' – sweets – *'suckshop'* – sweetshop.

'Taters' – potatoes.

'Tay' – tea.

'Tay on we' – it's not on us – often used as a police term to state that the incident is not within the boundaries of their local policing area.

'Trapes along' – walk aimlessly without a sense of purpose.

'Waggin it' – playing truant from school.

'Wench' – girl or young woman.

'Whale' – wheel or tyre.

'Whatsaname' – a name that can't be remembered.

'Yampy' – *'daft'* or stupid.

'Yed' – head.

'Yow' – you – *'yow alroight'* – you alright – *'Yow Am'* – you are.

5

COVENTRY AND WARWICKSHIRE SAYINGS

(With thanks to Barry Crowley)

'Away with the fairies' – eccentric – *'in another world'* – detached from reality.

'Batch' – small round loaf.

'Beduth' – Bedworth.

'Biffer' – someone considered to be ugly.

'Chuddy' – chewing gum.

'De-Di' – an ice-cream cone.

'Dillon' – used in Warwickshire to describe the *'runt of the litter'* or the smallest child in a family.

'Entry' – passageway between two terraced houses.

'Godcakes' – triangular pastries filled with mincemeat produced in Coventry.

'Hacked off' – annoyed.

'Jitty' – an alleyway in Bedworth.

'Lob' – throw.

'Mardy' – moody or *'stroppy'*.

'Noddy' – a condom.

'On the box' – *'on the panel'* – being sick from work or school with a certified doctor's note.

'Oojamacallit' or *'thingymybob'* – referring to someone whose name you have forgotten or *'thingamajig'* the name of something you can't remember.

'Ourgate and back' – people who couldn't take a holiday would use this phrase when referring to the fact that the furthest they would be going was to the end of their garden and back.

'Peeping Tom' – a voyeur – the only man to spy on Lady Godiva as she rode naked on a horse through Coventry.

'Pulled' – met someone for a romantic or sexual encounter.

'Pumps' – gym shoes or plimsolls.

'Ratted' – drunk.

'Sent to Coventry' – isolated or not spoken to – originates from the hostile reception given to Royalist prisoners held at St John's Church in Coventry during the English Civil War when Coventry was a Parliamentarian stronghold.

'Simmer Down' – calm down.

'Sprog' – baby.

'The Old Five' – an old nickname for Coventry City Football club.

'Treacle Town' – Nuneaton.

'Tuck' – sweets.

'Waggin it' – *'bunking off'* – playing truant from school.

'Whaddya reckon' – what do you think about that.

6

EAST MIDLANDS SAYINGS

'Ah'll sithee agen' – I'll see you again.

'Alrate youth' – alright young man – used in Nottingham.

'Am I heck as like' – what you said about me is untrue.

'As any onya any onya?' – have any of you got something that I need?

'Avya gorra wi'ya?' – is the wife with you?

'Ay up' – greeting – 'Ay up me duck' – used in Nottingham.

'Badly' – hungover.

'Belt job' – easy job.

'Blather-yeded' – silly person.

'Blortin' – crying.

'Bobbar' – please don't touch.

'Bobbos' – horses.

'Bonny' – looking well, sturdy or robust.

'Chuddie' – pants.

'Clouts' – trousers.

'Corsey' – pavement.

'Cos?' – can you?

'Cossie' – swimming costume.

'Croaker' – doctor.

'Dog shelf' – floor.

'Ducks necks' – bottle of lemonade.

'Fast' – stuck.

'Gizzabit' – let me have some.

'Me owd mucker' – greeting to an old friend.

'Mesen' – myself.

'My yard' – my house.

'Nesh' – a weak person.

'Now then' – greeting.

'Oakie' – ice-cream.

'Pot' – plaster cast.

'Stop your mythering' – stop *'whinging'* or complaining.

'Tabs' – ears.

'Thisens' – themselves, yourselves.

'Tuffees' – sweets.

'Ussens' – ourselves.

'Wazzerk' – fool.

'Y'usen' – yourself.

7

OTHER ENGLISH SAYINGS

'ACAB' – *'All Coppers Are Bastards'* – historically tattooed on the knuckles of some people with criminal records and frequently seen in prison.

'A bit of a shoeing' – *'a bloody nose'* – *'a bit of a duffing up'* – *'a good kicking'* – given a sharp lesson.

'A bit of how's your father' – sexual intercourse.

'At the end of your tether' – exhausted – can't go on.

'A Cracker' – outstanding – *'good looking'*.

'A Doozey' – an extraordinary one of its kind.

'Add fuel to the fire' – make something worse.

'Aerated' – over excited – upset or anxious.

'Always start the day off right' – *'start as you mean to go on'* – *'put your best foot forward'* – aim to do your best – be organised and positive.

'A stitch in time saves nine' – taking some form of action early on can save a lot more *'hassle'* in the future.

'A load of old tosh' – talking rubbish.

'A punt' – make a guess or a bet – take a chance.

'As mad as a box of frogs' – crazy.

'At loggerheads' – unable to agree – opposing views.

'Axe to grind' – strong opinion or predetermined agenda.

'Backed the right horse' – made the right choice.

'Baloney' – nonsense or falsehoods.

'Bang on' – exactly right.

'Barge in' – push in.

'Barking up the wrong tree' – making a mistake.

'Bazookas' – large breasts.

'Beer Goggles' – perception of reality effected by the supposed influence of alcohol.

'Beggars belief' – unbelievable.

'Being put through the wringer' – to be put under pressure.

'Belt' – hit someone – *'belt'* someone in the *'kisser'* – mouth.

'Better the devil you know than the devil you don't' – better to deal with a difficult person or situation you have experience of dealing with rather than the unknown which could be worse.

'Big Smoke' – London – *'down the smoke'*.

'Binned' – sacked – removed.

'Birds of a feather flock together' – like-minded people stick together.

'Blank canvas' – plenty of scope for filling in the detail – lots of opportunity to put a *'personal stamp'* on something.

'Blazing' – an attractive person.

'Blindsided' – didn't see it coming.

'Boss-eyed' – cross-eyed.

'Brass-necked' – shows no shame.

'Butter wouldn't melt in your mouth' – being overly coy or modest – cool.

'Canned up' – intoxicated, drunk.

'Canny' – shrewd, good, nice, lovely.

'Carping on about it' – finding fault, fussy, being critical about something.

'Carry the fire' – keep hope alive in a seemingly hopeless world.

'Catch your breath' – rest after exercise.

'Cat nap' – brief sleep.

'Cat's P**s' – a drink that tastes like something awful.

'Caught napping' – caught unawares, unprepared.

'Champing at the bit' – eager, keen to *'get on with it'*.

'Chat someone up' – talk informally to someone where there is normally an attraction.

'Chewing the fat' – talking about anything and everything – *'gossiping'* – *'small talk'*.

'Chivvy things along' – accelerate the progress of something.

'Claptrap' – nonsense.

'Close to the bone' – *'near to the mark'* – *'grating'* – a remark penetrating and accurate to the point of causing discomfort.

'Coalface' – *'at the sharp end'* dealing with things in an operational rather than strategic or managerial setting.

'Cocky' – *'full of oneself'* – brash, or over-confident.

'Coming up trumps' – *'smelling of roses'* – achieving a positive outcome – *'come up with the goods'* – *'played a blinder'*.

'Cop off' – sexual encounter.

'Coppers' – 'The Filfth' – 'Five-O' – 'The Old Bill' – 'Rozzers' – 'Pigs' – 'Bobbies' – 'Babylon' – 'The Thin Blue Line' – 'Johnny Law' – 'Bluebottles' – 'Fuzz' – 'Boys in Blue' – 'Peelers' – 'Plod' – 'Woodentops' – 'Dibble' – police officers. The Cornish word for police is 'Kreslu'.

'Cottoned on' – begin to understand.

'Cover all bases' – consider every option when planning.

'Crack on' – get going.

'Cut off your nose to spite the face' – a needlessly self-destructive over-reaction to a problem.

'Dead excited' – very excited.

'Dead Set' – determined.

'Damp Squib' – much less impressive than expected.

'Dapper' – smart.

'Deliver the goods' – complete the task.

'Different kettle of fish' – a completely different issue.

'Ditched' – abandoned or left.

'Do their legs' – do them a *'bad turn'* – *'chop their legs off at the knees'* – damage them – *'do the dirty'*.

'Doesn't give a toss' – cares less – not bothered.

'Done and dusted' – finished.

'Don't mince your words' – say what you mean – don't dilute the message.

'Don't poke your nose in' – don't interfere.

'Don't touch it with a barge pole' – have nothing to do with it.

'Doolally tap' – or *'tapped'* – crazy. Comes from a British Army phrase originating from a transit Camp in India called Deolali.

Soldiers waiting to go home used to go mad from boredom waiting around. They developed *'camp fever'* and *'lost their minds'*.

'Dot the eyes and cross the Ts' – pay attention to every detail.

'Double dip' – to take double than ones share – stealing.

'Dragged through a hedge backwards' – looking dishevelled or untidy.

'Drawn the short straw' – got the least favourable outcome in a situation.

'Dressed up like a dog's dinner' – over-dressed – extremely smart.

'Drive me around the bend' – make me crazy.

'Drop a clanger' – make a big mistake.

'Drop in the ocean' – insignificant amount, negligible.

'Drowning your sorrows' – having an alcoholic drink to feel better.

'Dutch man's uncle' – expression of surprise at something improbable.

'Eat humble pie' – *'eat your own words'* – apologise – accept that you are wrong.

'Empty vessels make the most noise' – those with the least knowledge and talent speak the loudest.

'Excuse the pun' – making use of an amusing word or phrase to make a point.

'Faffing about' – *'messing around'* – making a fuss.

'Finicky' – *'fussy'* or hard to please.

'Flowered it up a bit' – exaggerated.

'Foggiest idea' – no idea.

'For God's Sake' – an expression of anger, surprise, frustration or impatience – *'For Christs Sake'* – *'For Pete's Sake'* – an expression which is more than 100 years old.

'Front it' – face it – confront it *'head on'*.

'FTS' – 'f**k' the system.

'Gaffes' – *'off the cuff'* remarks which usually entail an element of *'putting your foot in it'* and causing some embarrassment.

'Gander' – look.

'Gene' – cool, crazy, insane, awesome.

'Geordie' – someone from the North East. The miners in that area used safety lamps designed by George Stephenson. The name is a derivation of the name *'George'*.

'Get down to brass tacks' – get to the point – *'the nub of the issue'* – important detail.

'Get their back up' – upset someone.

'Get wind of' – find something out.

'Gigolo' – a young man supported by a woman, typically older, to become her lover.

'Give it a good shot' – tried their best.

'Give someone a good drubbin' – give someone a beating.

'Go to pot' – *'go to seed'* – deteriorate.

'Gob' – mouth – *'gobby'* – mouthy.

'Gobstopper' – large, round, hard sweet.

'Gogglebox' – television set.

'Going bananas' – *'going ballistic'* – over excited and uncontrollable.

'Goosebumps' – a state of the skin caused by cold, fear or excitement leading to small raised areas and body hairs standing upright. To get this condition someone might be *'scared s**tless out of their wits'* or be *'as pleased as punch'* or *'like a dog with two d**ks'* or as cold as *'hell freezing over'*.

'Got the T-Shirt' – been there – done that!

'Grow a pair' – get some courage.

'Had it coming in spades' – thoroughly deserved something.

'Half-Cocked' – not ready or prepared – *'On a wing and a prayer'*.

'Hand Cranker' – someone self-opinionated with a high regard of themselves.

'Hanging around' – waiting.

'Happy as a lark' – contented – very happy – carefree – *'Happy as Larry'* – comes from Larry Foley an undefeated Australian boxer in the 1890s.

'Have your cake and eat it' – *'best of both worlds'* – to have or do two good things that are impossible to have or do at the same time.

'Having a cob on' – being unhappy and moody.

'Having a drag or puff' – smoking a cigarette or *'weed'* cannabis.

'Hit the sack' – go to bed.

'Hobson's Choice' – a free choice but no choice and one which you *'take or leave'*. Said to originate from Thomas Hobson – 1545 to 1631 who ran a thriving livery stable. He created a strict rotation system for his working horses so that the better ones were not overworked. You took the horse you got or got nothing at all.

'Horses for courses' – choosing the right person for a role or job based on them meeting the appropriate requirements.

'H'way the lads' – a term of encouragement used by *'Geordies'* in the North.

'Ifs, buts and maybes' – no clear decision, unclear, undecided, things left unanswered.

'In his oil tot' – feeling satisfied. From the days when working men had a tot of olive oil before drinking beer in the belief that it would put a lining on their stomachs and thus prevent them from getting drunk.

'In the ballpark' – in about the right place.

'In the club' – *'up the duff'* – pregnant.

'In the pipeline' – on the way – in the process of being planned.

'It's like corn in Egypt' – a *'biblical'* saying to indicate a plentiful supply of something.

'It was sick' – crazy, cool, insane.

'Jacked it in' – left – resigned – *'called it a day'*.

'Jacksy' – a person's bottom.

'Jarring' – annoying or disagreeable.

'Jekyll and Hyde' – split personality – one good and the other bad.

'Jocks' – a derogatory term for people from Scotland.

'Keeping your powder dry' – waiting for the right moment to take a course of action.

'Keep the lid on' – remain in control – keep a secret.

'Kicked the bucket' – died.

'Knackers' – testicles.

'Knee high to a grasshopper' – very small or young.

'Knickers in a twist' – get upset over something small.

'Know your onions' – know what you are talking about.

'Last nail in the coffin' – *'final straw'* – an inevitable outcome to a situation.

'Let sleeping dogs lie' – leave things as they are – *'don't open a can of worms'*.

'Like a red-rag to a bull' – trying to *'wind someone up'* or aggravate them.

'Likes the sound of their own voice' – Self-opinionated, pompous, self-centred.

'Loads' – a lot.

'LOB' – *'load of b****cks'* – nonsense.

'Lol' – laugh out loud. One of the most common slang terms in electronic communications.

'Loose Cannon' – unpredictable.

'Losing your touch' – no longer doing something as well as you could before.

'Lost a shilling and found a penny' – lost something of value and found something of lower value.

'Lost their marbles' – *'lost the plot'* – gone a bit crazy – *'Barking'* mad – *'Off his Rocker'*.

'Lump together' – create one, join, stick together.

'Make it snappy' – make it quick.

'Many a good tune played on an old man's fiddle' – older age is not a barrier to still being very good at doing something.

'Many a slip twixt cup and lip' – things can still go wrong even when the outcome does not look in doubt.

'Meat Wagon' – an old term for a police van.

'Mickey Dripping' – a nickname given to someone with the Christian name Michael in the 1970s. Some say it originates in the North West. Dripping was a form of *'lard'* and one more adventurous theory is that it originates from Irish men who in the 1800s used lard to smarten their hair or splashed Holy Water on themselves hence 'dripping'. Surnames also featured with word association so for example anyone called Clark became known as *'Nobby'* and anyone with the surname White was called *'Chalky'*.

'Morning Glory' – the type of erection a man can get first thing in the morning after sleeping – thought to be because of having a full bladder.

'Moving heaven and earth' – doing their utmost.

'Muck it up' – 'make a mess' – do something badly, inept.

'My shout' – my turn to buy a round of drinks.

'Neck it' – 'down in one' – drink in one go quickly – normally alcohol.

'Netflix and Chill' – urban slang for have sex.

'Never judge a book by its cover' – don't just go by first impressions of outward appearance alone.

'Never the twain shall meet' – not possible to reach an agreement – two things too different to exist alongside each other.

'Nincompoop' – a silly or stupid person.

'Nitty Gritty' – getting into detail. Said to have its origins from the days of slave traders referring to the removal of *'nits'* and *'grit'* from the heads of slaves being transported.

'No s**t Sherlock' – a sarcastic remark to someone who has just stated the obvious – the person on the receiving end can defend themselves by responding **'F**k you Watson'**.

'Nail it' – prove something, achieve something.

'Not the foggiest' – no idea – *'not a clue'*.

'Nothing off the table' – all options open.

'Nothing ventured, nothing gained' – *'speculate to accumulate'* – give it a try although success is not pre-ordained.

'Off you trot' – go now!

'Old Codger' – older person.

'Old as Methuselah' – extremely old – from the Old Testament – Methuselah was said to be the world's oldest living human being.

'Old crate' – rickety old vehicle – usually a car or a plane.

'Olive Branch' – a peace offering to bring a dispute or argument to an end.

'OMG' – *'Oh my God'* – an expression of surprise or exclamation.

'On a bender' – getting drunk – *'on the lash'*.

'Onwards and upwards' – make progress – move forwards.

'On the Square' – a Freemason.

'One for the road' – the last alcoholic drink before leaving from somewhere.

'Organ Grinder not the monkey' – I want to speak to the person in charge not the *'hired hand'*.

'Paddies' – a derogatory term for people from Ireland.

'Paid the price' – suffered the consequences.

'Painting the town red' – going out to have a very good entertaining and lively time.

'Passing like ships in the night' – never see each other.

'Patter' – talk.

'Pear shaped' – gone wrong.

'Peeing in the same pot' – all in something together – a joint enterprise.

'Pigs might fly' – it's impossible.

'Pinky Promise' – a traditional gesture among young children involving the locking of two little fingers to signify that a promise has been made which should not be broken.

'Pipe Up – or down' – speak up – be quiet.

'Playing cupid' – bringing two people together for romantic purposes.

'Plonk' – wine.

'Pop her cherry' – the breaking of a female's hymen through a sexual act. Losing one's virginity.

'Pop off' – leave, depart, die – *'popped his clogs'*.

'Poppycock' – originates from a Dutch dialect word meaning *'soft poop'* – or *'doll excrement'* – talking *'crap'* or rubbish.

'Practice what you preach' – do the things that you advise others to do.

'Proof of the pudding is in the eating' – you will only know if something is good by trying it.

'Pull a fast one' – *'play a stroke'* – play an unfair trick.

'Pull your act together' – get organised to become effective.

'Push the boat out' – originates from sailors on shore-leave during the 1930s – to buy a round of drinks.

'Put a foot in it' – act without thinking – *'put your size nines in'* – a lack of thought as to your actions.

'Put a sock in it' – be quiet – shut up – enough!

'Put a spanner in the works' – *'upset the applecart'* – throw an issue or a problem into something or a plan which has already been sorted out and agreed in principle.

'Put a sticking plaster over it' – applying a short-term solution to a problem.

'Put your money where your mouth is' – show by actions and not just words.

'Quick Snifter' – a small alcoholic drink – *'a short'* – usually a whisky or something similar.

'Quirky' – different in a pleasing way.

'Raggedy Arsed' – clothing in poor condition.

'Rings a bell' – means something.

'Rock the boat' – create a problem, cause upset.

'Rough it' – live without possessions or *'creature comforts'* that you might normally have.

'Scoff' – eat quickly.

'Scram' – *'skedaddle'* – go away – *'get lost'*.

'Scratch the surface' – take a superficial look at something.

'Scupper things' – *'sink'* an idea or course of action.

'See a man about a dog' – a phrase used to conceal one's true destination.

'See you later' – a friendly goodbye but not to be taken too literally. There is generally no intention of seeing the person later.

'Seize the day' – capture the moment, take the initiative.

'Shades' – sunglasses.

'Shafted' – *'had over'* – being treated unfairly or badly by another person.

'Shambles' – a mess – disorganised.

'Shed load' – lots.

'S****t hits the fan'** – a situation which suddenly explodes and causes a lot of trouble for someone.

'S****t Off'** – an alternative way of telling someone more politely to *'go away'*.

'Short and curlies' – *'by the balls'* – referring to pubic hair – under complete control.

'Shut the front door!' – express surprise.

'Side-lined' – put into a lesser influential position.

'Six of one and half a dozen of the other' – *'nothing to write home about'* – *'a fuss about nothing'* – *'a storm in a teacup'* – a situation which has been created of higher proportions than it should be.

'Six of the best' – six strokes of the cane as a punishment – historically common in boy's schools.

'Skinny dipping' – swimming naked – *'starkers'* – *'in the noddy'*.

'Skiver' – lazy person.

'Slow burn' – a gradual build-up over a period.

'Slowly, slowly, catchie monkey' – do not be too hasty – being patient will serve you better.

'Small fry' – not important – *'lower down the pecking order'* – *'lower down the food chain'*.

'Smoggies' – people from the Teeside area of the UK.

'Someone just walked over my grave' – something made me shiver or shudder unexpectedly.

'Something smells fishy' – doesn't feel or seem quite right – *'something's up'* – *'smell a rat'*.

'Something for the weekend' – a condom.

'Something tucked up my sleeve' – ideas or plans not yet shared with others – an *'ace card'* or *'trick up your sleeve'*.

'Sparko' – *'spark out'* – unconscious.

'Spin on that' – with a finger in the air – decline to do something.

'Straw that broke the camel's back' – a seemingly minor thing or action that results in a larger response taking place due to its accumulative effect.

'Stone the crows' – expressing incredulity or disbelief.

'Stupid Norbert' – a fool.

'Sucking a Lemon' – you look like you've got a sour or miserable face. A grimace emanating from being *'fed up'*.

'Taffs' – a derogatory term for people from Wales.

'Tats' – tattoos.

'Take the bull by the horns' – take control or action – grip a situation – *'grasp the nettle'* – do something.

'Tell a whopper' – a big lie.

'That's sick' – insane, crazy – *'cool'* – *'wicked'*.

'The Dragon' – the wife.

'The better end of the stick' – the better option, the better deal, the better result.

'The flicks' – the cinema.

'The jury is still out' – undecided, a decision not reached, still under consideration.

'The old grey matter' – the brain.

'The Woo' – people from Worcester.

'Thick as a plank' – stupid.

'Throw the towel in' – give up – the act of ceding defeat in boxing.

'Tie a knot in your handkerchief' – remind yourself to do something.

'TLC' – Tender Loving Care.

'Touch base' – make contact.

'Touching someone up' – indecent assault – inappropriate behaviour.

'Treading water' – not moving forward, static, not making any progress, going nowhere.

'Trigger happy' – too *'quick off the mark'* – not thinking before responding, impulsive.

'Trousers at half-mast' – worn higher up the leg and waist than normal, exposing the ankles.

'Turn a blind eye' – ignore something.

'Turn up the heat' – increase the level of activity to achieve something.

'Turning the tables' – changing a situation to your advantage.

'Uncle Tom Cobley and all' – a long list of people. The phrase comes from a Devon folk song *'Widecombe Fair'*.

'Under wraps' – kept secret.

'Up in the air' – left in obeyance, not resolved, undecided.

'Up the road' – somewhere not that far away.

'Up the swanny' – *'up the creek without a paddle'* – *'hit a dead-end'* – in serious trouble, hopeless situation.

'Up to snuff' – *'cut the mustard'* – an applicable standard.

'Up to your eyeballs' – in deep or fully immersed or busy with something.

'Use a sprat to catch a mackerel' – take a small risk to achieve a bigger outcome.

'Verbal Diarrhoea' – talk too much – incessantly.

'Wagged' – play truant from school.

'Walk on eggshells' – be extremely cautious about your words or actions – generally to ensure not causing offence or upset to someone. Often used in bereavement situations.

'Walk on water' – to do something impossible or extraordinary – the phrase originates from a story in the Gospel about Jesus.

'Waste of space' – useless or incompetent.

'Water under the bridge' – it's finished, it's in the past and no longer to be regarded as important.

'Went a purler' – tripped or fallen.

'Went up in a puff of smoke' – disappeared.

'Wet blanket' – lacks assertion – indecisive – *'soft'* – weak, not commanding any sense of authority or respect.

'Wet the baby's head' – consume an alcoholic drink to celebrate the birth of a child.

'What a tool' – referring to person who is foolish – a bit of an idiot – useless.

'What's the goss' – what's the gossip.

'Whoops-a-daisy' – an exclamation of surprise – normally when someone falls over.

'Winging it' – trying to do something whilst unprepared for the task – *'chancing it'*.

'White elephant' – an expensive project or experience which at the end of the day has no great worth or value.

'White smoke' – a way of saying that a group has reached a consensus or agreement.

'Wild goose chase' – a fruitless search or effort.

'Wobbly' – not committed – uncertain – unsure.

'Woke' – aware or informed in a political or cultural sense.

'Writing on the wall' – clear signs of an inevitable outcome.

'Wrong end of the stick' – a misunderstanding.

'X-Ray Eyes' – *'seeing through things'* that no-one else can and coming to a conclusion based on that vision.

'Yonks' – years.

'Zippy' – fast, speedy – *'Speedy Gonzales'*.

'Zzzs' – snoring – or to *'catch some zzzs'* – get some sleep.

SOME BRISTOL PHRASES

(With thanks to Nicki Layton & Amy Watkins)

'Aarsh' – harsh.

'Ackrut' – accurate.

'Ark at ee' – check you out.

'Asdal' – Asda supermarket.

'Babber' – baby – a term of endearment.

'Baff' – Bath – an ancient City south-west of Bristol.

'Bristolian' – someone from Bristol.

'Brizzle' – Bristol.

'Cacks' – underwear.

'Cheers drive' – thanks for the lift.

'Churz' – cheers!

'Come tight' – that hurt.

'Coopy down' – crouch down.

'Daps' – plimsolls.

'Fanks' – thank you.

'Fink' – think.

'Gashead' – Bristol Rovers football fan.

'Gert lush' – really good – lovely.

'Ginormous' – smaller than gigantic but bigger than enormous.

'Glider' – cider.

'Inchew' – aren't you.

'Jasper' – a wasp.

'Keener' – someone who is clever.

'Lackey band' – elastic band.

'Me Lover' – *'alright me lover'* – a term of endearment.

'Mind' – take care or be careful – used to emphasise a point.

'Nerr' – never.

'Ow bist?' – how are you?

'Peepaw' – people.

'Pizzal' – pizza.

'Raggy' – hand-rolled cigarette.

'Slider' – playground slide.

'Smooth' – *'smoothing a dog'* – stroke.

'Snow is pitching' – the snow is settling on the ground.

'Topper' – crust – end piece of a loaf of bread.

'Wells' – Wales.

'Wesson' – Weston Super Mare.

'Yewman' – human.

'Zider' – cider.

9

RHYMING 'COCKNEY' SLANG

Originates from early 19th century
in the East End of London.

'Adam and Eve, it' – believe it.

'A la mode' – code.

'Apples and Pears' – stairs.

'April Fool' – stool or tool.

'Argy Bargy' – trouble.

'Bag of Sand' – £1,000.

'Barnet Fair' – hair.

'Barry McGuigan' – *'big un'* acting in a *'cocky'* or bullying manner.

'Bins' – spectacles.

'Bird Lime' – doing time in prison.

'Bluebrick' – *'nick'* – police station.

'Bottle Stopper' – *'copper'* – police officer.

'Brown Bread' – dead.

'Chalk Farm' – arm.

'Custard and Jelly' – *'telly'* – television.

'Daisy roots' – boots.

'Deep Sea Diver' – *'fiver'* – £5.

'Dog and bone' – phone.

'Emma Freuds' – haemorrhoids.

'Flowery Dell' – cell.

'Frog and Toad' – road.

'Grasshopper' – copper – police officer.

'Gregory Peck' – neck.

'Have a butchers (hook)' – take a look.

'Have a Turkish Bath' – have a laugh.

'Him Indoors' – husband.

'Huge plates of meat' – large feet.

'I suppose' – nose.

'Jack Jones' – alone.

'Jam Jar' – car.

'Jekyll and Hyde's' – *'strides'* – trousers or *'Jekyll and Hyde'* – snide or fake.

'Jimmy Riddle' – *'piddle'* – *'pee'* – urinate.

'Kettle and Hob' – *'fob'* – watch.

'Khyber Pass' – *'ass'* – backside.

'Loaf of bread' – head.

'Mutton and Jeff' – deaf.

'North and South' – mouth.

'One and t'Other' – brother.

'Pin Pegs' – legs.

'Polo Mint' – *'skint'* – *'broke'* – penniless or *'Boracic Lint'* – *'skint'*.

'Pony and Trap' – *'crap'* – rubbish.

'Porkie Pies' – lies.

'Queens Park Ranger' – stranger.

'Rabbit and Pork' – talk.

'Rosie Lee' – tea.

'Ruby Murray' – curry.

'Salmon and Trout' – *'snout'* – informant.

'Skin and blister' – one's sister.

'Sweaty sock' – *'Jock'* – a Scottish person.

'Sweeney Todd' – Flying Squad in the Metropolitan Police.

'Tea Leaf' – thief.

'Tin Lid' – *'kid'* – child.

'Tin Tack' – sack.

'Tit for Tat' – *'Titfer'* – hat.

'Tom and Dick' – sick.

'Treacle Tart' – sweetheart.

'Trouble and Strife' – wife.

'Turtle Dove' – love.

'Uncle Ned' – head.

'Vera Lynn' – chin – gin.

'Whistle and Flute' – suit.

'You're having a giraffe' – *'having a laugh'* – joking.

'Yul Bryner' – dinner.

A BIT MORE LONDON SLANG

'Alie' – I agree.

'Bait' – obvious.

'Bangin' – good.

'Beef' – hostility between two people.

'Blud/Blad' – brother/friend.

'Bovvered' – interested.

'Chirpsing' – flirting.

'Cretin' – idiot.

'Dapper' – smart.

'Dizzy' – crazy.

'Dry' – boring.

'Ends' – area or neighbourhood.

'Fresh' – looks good.

'Feds' – police – *'Jakes'*.

'Garms' – clothing.

'Heads' – people.

'Hype' – too much.

'In it' – isn't it.

'Jam' – relax.

'Links' – get together with someone.

'Monkey' – £500.

'Marvin' – hungry.

'On top' – situation gets out of hand.

'Rinsed' – overused.

'Taxed' – stealing.

'Tight' – cheap.

'Treck' – something far away.

'Wicked' – cool.

'Wifey' – girlfriend.

'Younger' – sibling.

10

SLANG FROM MANCHESTER

'Anging' – disgusting.

'Bagsy' – I want it.

'Bang out of order' – not the done thing.

'Bangin' – good.

'Barm Cake' – soft roll – also known as a *'chip barm'*.

'Bins' – spectacles.

'Brew' – cup of tea.

'Burst on your banjo' – *'let off steam'* – *'let your hair down'* – party.

'Cadge' – *'scrounge'* – get something for nothing.

'Champers' – champagne – *'shampoo'*.

'Chinnies' – lies.

'Chuffed' – pleased.

'Cock' – *'mate'* – *'pal'* – friend.

'Corporation Pop' – water.

'Daft ha'p'orth' – stupid.

'Dead' – very.

'Decka' – take a look.

'Dinner Medals' – food stains on clothing after eating.

'Gagging' – thirsty.

'Gill' – half a pint.

'Gruds' – underpants.

'Is it ek as like' – no it's not.

'Kecks' – trousers – *'trolleys'*.

'Kippered' – exhausted.

'Leathered' – drunk – *'off yer trolley'*.

'Mad fer it' – to be excited.

'Mancunian' – *'Manc'* – person from Manchester.

'Mingin' – disgusting.

'Mint' – very good.

'Nippers' – *'kids'* – children.

'Nowty' – *'grumpy'* – moody.

'Numpty' – stupid.

'Obstropolous' – awkward – *'stroppy'*.

'On the lash' – drinking alcohol.

'On't blower' – on the telephone.

'Our kid' – sibling.

'Pop' – fizzy drink.

'Put slap on' – apply make-up.

'Round our way' – where we live.

'Scran' – food, snack.

'Scrote' – anti-social person.

'Sharabang' – coach.

'Sherbert' – alcoholic drink.

'Shrike' – cry out, scream, *'yell'*.

'Skenning' – looking.

'Skinheads on rafts' – beans on toast.

'Slaphead' – bald.

'Smashed' – high on drugs.

'Sound' – good.

'Stush' – acting superior.

'Sucking your face' – *'snogging'* – kissing.

'Sup up' – drink up.

'Swede' – head.

'Take a chill pill' – calm down.

'Top Banana' – *'cool'* – *'wicked'* – great.

'Up the dancers' – up the stairs.

'Yer Wot' – excuse me!

'Yonner' – someone up yonder – north.

RHYMING SLANG USED IN MANCHESTER

'Bobbins (Of Cotton)' – *'rotten'* – really bad.

'Bell (Ringers)' – fingers.

'Claire (Raynors)' – trainers.

'Gorton (Tank)' – bank.

'Hankin (Marvin)' – *'Starvin'* – hungry.

'Newton (Heath)' – teeth.

'Orange (Wash)' – squash.

'Orchestra (Stalls)' – balls.

'**Salford (Docks)**' – socks.

'**Standat (Ease)**' – cheese.

'**Trafford (Park)**' – Mark.

'**Whalley (Range)**' – change.

11

MERSEYSIDE SLANG AND SAYINGS

'Antwacky' – out of date.

'Bevied' – drunk.

'Bifter' – cigarette.

'Bird' – woman.

'Chocker' – busy.

'Devvoed' – devastated.

'Eee' – an expression of disgust.

'Gorra cob on' – annoyed.

'G'Wed' – go ahead.

'Hurry Up Van' – police van.

'Jarg' – fake.

'Lacka' – hair spray.

'Lah' – friend.

'Lecky' – electricity – commonly used in Liverpool – a *'scouse'* word.

'Lemo' – controlled drugs.

'Made Up' – very happy – best thing ever.

'Ozzy' – hospital.

'Paddy Wagon' – a historical reference to many of the officers and prisoners in Liverpool being Irish.

'Queen' – girlfriend.

'Scouser' – someone from Liverpool.

'Scran' – food.

'Scuffer' – police officer.

'Snide' – not being nice to someone.

'Sound' – good.

'Swerve' – avoid.

'The Bizzies' – a derogatory term for the police – created following a perception that the police were always too busy to assist with minor crime matters.

'Wack' – friend – *'wacker'* – also used in the Midlands.

'Webs' – shoes.

'Wool' – not a true *'Liverpudlian'*.

12

YORKSHIRE SAYINGS

'Aye' – yes.

'Appen' – possibly.

'Allus' – always.

'Ba'ht' – to be without.

'Beck' – a stream or creek of water.

'Black Leg' – someone who doesn't go on strike when one is called.

'Butty' – sandwich.

'Champion' – excellent.

'Climmin' – an old Yorkshire phrase for cliff climbing.

'Dale' – the valley.

'Dee Dah' – a person from Sheffield.

'Dillons' – a bit dim or stupid.

'Ey up' – a common greeting or used to express concern.

'Faffin' – messing around.

'Flummoxed' – disorganised or confused.

'Ginnel' – an alleyway.

'Gip' – vomit.

'Hear all, see all say nowt, eat all sup all say nowt, and if thee do out for nowt do it for thee sen' – nothing for nothing unless you are doing it for yourself.

'Hell Fire' – an expression of disbelief.

'If in doubt do nowt' – if you are not sure do nothing.

'Jammy' – got lucky.

'Jiggered' – worn out.

'Kegs' – trousers.

'Larking around' – playing around.

'Lugs' – hair tangles and knots.

'Manky' – revolting.

'Mardy' – grumpy.

'Monk on' – ill-tempered.

'Narky' – bad tempered or moody.

'Nowt' – nothing.

'Ow do' – how are you doing?

'Owt' – anything.

'Pack it in' – stop it.

'Parky' – chilly.

'Push Iron' – bicycle.

'Rig-welted' – a sheep that gets stuck lying on its back.

'Snicket' – an alley.

'Sprog' – a young child.

'Snek Lifter' – a pint of beer.

'Swill' – take a drink.

'Tha' – you.

'Tyke' – an insulting word for a Yorkshire person.

'Twonk' – an insult referring to a person being stupid.

'Un' – one.

'Vexed' – angry.

'Wang' – throw something.

'Watter' – water.

'Wasak' – idiot.

'Yacker' – an acre of land.

'Yam' – home.

'Yonder' – distance.

SHEFFIELD SAYINGS

'Agen' – against.

'Ah' – yes.

'Beck' – stream.

'Breadcake' – bread roll.

'Cooking on Gas' – making good progress.

'Courting' – dating – *'seeing someone'*.

'De Dah' – a person from Sheffield.

'Gipping' – vomiting.

'Give Over' – shut up.

'Love' – a greeting to males or females.

'Mash' – making tea in a teapot after the water is added.

'More fat on a chip' – slim or skinny.

'Nesh' – cold.

'Now then' – conversation starter.

'Pranny' – idiot or fool.

'Reyt' – right.

'Sneck' – nose.

'Somert' – something.

'Spice' – sweets.

'Togger' – football.

'Yourn' – yours.

13

SAYINGS FROM OTHER UK COUNTRIES

NORTHERN IRISH SAYINGS

'A fair whack' – a reasonable share.

'Across the Water' – referring to England or the rest of the UK.

'Acting the lig' – fooling around.

'Bake' – mouth.

'Baltic' – freezing cold.

'Banjaxed' – broken.

'Beezer' – super.

'Beg' – bag.

'Belfast Milly' – from the 19th century – a mill worker – usually a young working-class woman.

'Black Maria' – police van used to transport prisoners.

'Blarney' – talk which aims to charm, flatter or persuade.

'Bob's your uncle' – and there it is – *'it's done'*.

'Boggin' – filthy.

'Boking' – not the most pleasant thing – vomiting.

'Bout ye?' – how are you?

'Brave' – a lot.

'Bucketin' – raining heavily.

'Buck eejit' – a term of endearment for someone who is silly.

'Cack attack' – become extremely nervous.

'Carry Out' – takeaway alcohol – usually from the *'offy'* – off-licence.

'Cat' – very bad.

'Courting' – dating.

'Crabbed' – irritable or bad-tempered.

'Craic' – having fun, party – *'a good craic'*.

'Dab-hand' – does a good job.

'Dander' – stroll or aimless wander.

'Dead on' – *'grand'* or *'cool'*.

'Dillon' – like a lion – loyal.

'Do you think I came up the Lagan in a bubble?' – used in Belfast – *'do you think I was born yesterday?'* – refers to the River Lagan in Northern Ireland. Basically means 'do you think I'm stupid?'

'Eariwig' – to listen to someone else's conversation.

'Eejit' – idiot.

'Faffin' – wasting time.

'GAWA' – *'Green and White Army'* – N.I. football supporters.

'Go for a poke' – go for an ice-cream.

'Gurn' – *'moan'* – complain about someone.

'Harpin on' – carry on discussing something that's already been resolved.

'Immersion' – home heating boiler system.

'Kitter-handed' – left-handed.

'Luckpenny' – a small discount on goods requested by the purchaser.

'McCooeys' – or *'Dunchers'* – people from Belfast.

'Mucker' – friend.

'No bother' – no trouble whatsoever.

'On the sauce bottle' – purchased through hire purchase (HP).

'Piggin' – filthy.

'Right' – time to go.

'Scundered' – embarrassed or mortified.

'Steamin' – drunk.

'Suckin diesel' – an improving situation.

'Thingy' – the person whose name has been forgotten.

'Town' – the city-centre.

'Wee' – small.

'What about ye?' – how are you?

'Wick' – rubbish.

'Wind your neck in' – shut up.

'Wise Up' – stop being stupid – come to your senses.

SCOTTISH SAYINGS
(With thanks to Gordon Padfield for his contribution)

'A Kent face' – a known person.

'Andy Murray' – curry.

'Auld' – old.

'Aye' – yes.

'Ba-hair' – a unit of measurement which is indeterminate – *'ball hair'* – pubic hair.

'Bahoochie' – bottom or *'bum'*.

'Banger' – a volatile individual.

'Bairn' – child or *'wain'*.

'Bevvy' – alcoholic drink.

'Bladdered' – *'hammered'* – *'blootered'* – *'rat-arsed'* – drunk.

'Blether' – *'chatterbox'* – talks incessantly.

'Boke' – gag or vomit.

'Braw' – men.

'Buttery' – a phrase used in Aberdeen for a bread roll.

'Cannae' – cannot.

'Canny' – colourful, clever or cautious.

'Chitter' – shiver.

'Clootie' – a piece of cloth.

'Corned beef' – deaf.

'Crabbit' – bad-tempered or *'grumpy'*.

'Dinna' – don't – *'dinna fash'* – don't worry.

'Dons' – people from Aberdeen – *'Aberdonians'*.

'Driech' – dreary weather.

'Drookit' – soaking wet.

'Fas' – a tassel or thing of little value.

'Feartie' – cow.

'Finicky' – fussy.

'Frae' – from.

'Gan' – going.

'Gie him the jail' – arrest him.

'Glaiket' – stupid.

'Glasgow kiss' – a sudden headbutt to the nose.

'Glaswegians' – people from Glasgow.

'Gloaming' – twilight or dusk.

'Haver' – talk rubbish.

'Hen' – female.

'He's a breach' – meaning likely the behaviour constitutes a *'breach of the peace'* which in Scotland carries far more punitive elements other than that of being *'bound over'* in England and Wales.

'Howlin' – smelly.

'Humongous' – huge.

'I'll gie ye a skelpit lug' – I'll give you a slap on the ear.

'Ken' – know.

'Lorraine Kelly' – *'telly'* – television.

'Mick Jagger' – Lager.

'Naff' – boring.

'Nane' – none.

'Patter' – talk fast.

'Peely Wally' – looking pale or ill.

'Polis' – police.

'Quaik' – tremble.

'Sassenachs' – an offensive term to describe English people.

'Skinny Malinky Longlegs' – a tall thin person.

'Scrabby' – dirty.

'Skelp' – slap.

'Smoorich' – kiss.

'Steamin' – drunk.

'Swally' – alcoholic drink.

'Taps off' – hot weather – *'tops off'*.

'Tartan Army' – Scotland football supporters.

'Tattie' – potato.

'Tidy' – women.

'Tube' – idiot.

'Wabbit' – tired.

'Wee' – little.

'Wee Barra' – a small person who people like.

'Wee dram' – small whiskey.

'Widnae' – wouldn't.

'Yaldi' – expressing excitement.

'You can't break a stick in a bundle' – a group of people co-operating can succeed in a situation where an individual cannot.

WELSH SAYINGS

'A Turk' – a nickname for someone from Llanelli.

'Cofi' – Caernarfon.

'cwtch' – safe place – cupboard.

'Dai Bach' – toilets.

'Dylan' – *'son of the sea'* – the most popular name in Wales for baby boys in 2010.

'From the Valleys' – a phrase used by people from Cardiff when referring to residents of parts of South Wales within the valley areas.

'How's it going butt?' – are you well my friend?

'It's nobbling out' – it's really cold outside.

'Lechyd da!' – good health – often heard at rugby matches.

'Lush' – short for luscious.

'Mun' – a word that doesn't mean anything but is used to place emphasis on another word used.

'Now in a minute' – on the way but not quite yet.

'Pob lwc' – good luck.

'Poor dab' – a misfortune has befallen someone.

'Popty Ping' – a microwave – an oven that goes *'ping'*.

'There we are then' – when a solution or proposal is presented as a *'done deal'* you aren't wholly happy about. It would be expressed in a disgruntled or dismissive tone.

'Twp' – a bit simple.

'Where to are you?' – where are you?

'Ych a Fi' – *'yuck'* – *'gross'* – that's disgusting.

14

SAYINGS AND SLANG FROM OTHER COUNTRIES

AMERICAN SLANG

'A real bummer' – an unpleasant or disappointing situation.

'Bail' or *'Ditch'* – break or cancel plans with someone.

'Chill' – calm down.

'Down to earth' – someone who is humble and easy to speak with.

'Feds' – the Federal Bureau of Investigation or United States Marshalls Service.

'Gee Whiz' – began life as a shortened version of *'Jesus'* – cut to *'gee'* – an expression of amazement.

'Here is the tea' – this is the news or latest gossip.

'It frosts my jaw' – it is really, really irritating.

'Looking for snow in the middle of July' – trying to make something out of the impossible.

'Monday morning Quarterbacking' – being wise after the event – every Quarterback can make the right pass after they have watched replays. Hence Monday morning decisions are always in hindsight.

'Sidewalk' – a paved path for pedestrians at the side of the road.

'Slay' – doing well.

'Uncle Sam' – the US Government – came into use in 1812 and thought to refer to Samuel Wilson.

'What's good?' – *'what's up?'* – how are you?

'Zap' – cook food quickly in a microwave.

AUSTRALIAN SAYINGS

'Ambo' – ambulance.

'Barbie' – BBQ.

'Bevvies' – alcoholic drinks.

'Bloke' – man.

'Chocker' – full.

'Coldie' – a beer.

'Down Under' – Australia or New Zealand.

'Eski' – fridge.

'Fair dinkum' – the truth.

'G' Day mate' – hello friend.

'Hit the frog and toad' – better get going.

'I reckon' – absolutely.

'In the drink' – in the water.

'Mozzies' – mosquitoes.

'Pressies' – presents.

'Sheila' – girl or young woman.

'Slab' – a pack of beers.

'Stinker of a day' – hot.

'*Sunnies*' – sunglasses.

'*Take a squiz*' – have a look.

'*The Wallabies*' – the national rugby team of Australia.

'*Trackies*' – track-suit trousers.

'*Tucker*' – food.

'*You Beauty*' – that's great.

CYPRIOT SAYINGS

(Contributions from Androulla (Andry) Christou-Layton,
Niki Ioannou Christou and Marios Christou)

'*Afendi*' – the master.

'*Ate them like a lettuce*' – dealt with the competition.

'*Bean by bean the bag is full*' – little by little you start small but eventually will achieve something bigger.

'*Become wind and smoke*' – disappear.

'*Brought their miles*' – recover or come to their senses.

'*Catch my leg*' – make a mistake.

'*Chinese*' – the nickname for Omonia football supporters – a reference to the club being well supported.

'*Cuts and sews*' – decides on their own without asking anyone.

'*For the favour of the flower the pot got watered*' – for the sake of love for someone that person's family are accepted as well.

'*Grass looks greener on the other side*' – an assumption that things will always be better somewhere else – does not always turn out to be true. (Also used in the UK).

'*Heavier than iron – sweeter than honey – can't be caught by hand or put in the pocket*' – sleep.

'*He/she will break from their bad feelings*' – someone who can't cope – very upset – jealous.

'*His brain is a field full of weeds*' – his head is '*full of rubbish*'.

'*Is a shovel*' – doesn't understand anything.

'*Is totally a brick*' – '*brainless*' – stupid.

'*It's a sea*' – it's a mess.

'*Kick the bucket*' – to die (also used in the UK).

'*Lost his watermelon*' – lost his mind – '*lost a screw*' – '*a screw loose somewhere*'.

'*Mbatsos*' – '*ice cream men*' – the police.

'*MMAD*' – public order trained police officers in the Republic of Cyprus Police – '*Motorised Direct-Action Unit*'.

'*Once here and once there*' – '*blows with the wind*' – unstable character.

'*Opened mouth but ate from the tongue*' – a lot of murmuring.

'*OI!*' – no! – a slang version of the Greek word '*ohi*'.

'*Patronos*' – a man of the night who '*sells women*'.

'*Pekse pellon*' – play crazy – ignore it or leave it.

'*Promised ovens and dry breads*' – words of '*air*' – false promises.

'*Saw death naked*' – very frightened.

'*SBAs*' – Sovereign Base Areas of Akrotiri and Dhekalia.

'*Sit, donkey, die*' – waiting a long time.

'Skata' – s**t – made a mess.

'Sleep good weather' – sleep without worries.

'Stayed on the shelf' – unmarried.

'Take all the oil' – remove all of someone's energy or strength.

'The crazy comes out eating or singing' – someone with no worries leaves the house with a full stomach or singing.

'The debt collector is calling me' – 'the 100' – I need to go to the toilet.

'The lid slid and found the pot' – they match each other.

'The man who sold a donkey saddle' – someone who betrays you is not worth more than a donkey saddle.

'The money is the nature of power' – in the end money dictates everything.

'The Moufflons' – the national rugby team of Cyprus.

'The wiser thing to do is to cook before you get hungry' – be prepared to do something to avoid a situation – be organised.

'They give the stale bread to the ones who don't have teeth with which to chew' – you don't know how to appreciate what you have until you no longer have the means to appreciate it.

'What he/she remembers in their brain makes them happy' – someone who makes themselves happy simply by having a sense of imagination rather than reality.

'Where am I waving to you, and where are you going' – not concentrating or misunderstanding.

'Where the Bishop goes on his own' – the toilet.

'You came from your own house now' – you don't believe me when I tell you something but when someone else tells you the same thing you believed them.

'You do midnight' – someone who has no idea.

'You have a label and someone who doesn't know you will buy you expensive' – you show something else of what you really are.

'You've seen the sweetness now that you have tasted the bitterness' – you appreciate the good having now seen what the bad looks like.

A CZECH SAYING

'Benga' – a slang word for police officers from the Romani word *'beng'* meaning *'devil'* or *'satan'*.

PHRASES USED IN EGYPT
(With thanks to Loukia Christou-Hawas and Samir Hawas)

'Akeed' – sure – yes of course.

'Bi Sharafak' – express disbelief.

'Estabena?' – do we agree?

'Fakes' – forget it or let it go.

'Horokrok' – barely.

'Inshallah' – God willing – it's out of my hands.

'Kawnaz' – someone whose mind *'goes blank'* – can't remember something.

'Khallas' – stop talking – give me some peace.

'**Kol Hawa**' – a derogatory term for *'shut up'*.

'**Mashallah**' – complementing something beautiful.

'**Mezaqtat**' – extremely happy.

'**Robabekya**' – Italian origin – old items which can be resold.

'**Sabah al Kheir**' – good morning – *'you have awoken'*.

'**Sabbooba**' – a reward.

'**Seeka**' – a short while.

'**Shaku Maku?**' – originates from Iraq – 'what's up?'

'**Shibshib**' – flipflops.

'**Tabtab**' – Coptic origin – patting or stroking.

'**Wallah**' – I swear to God.

'**Washwasha**' – whispering or speaking softly.

'**Ya Haram**' – express sympathy.

'**Ya Lahwi!**' – Oh my God! – *'Ya Rab'* – My God!

'**Ya Rayyal**' – express frustration.

'**Yallah**' – let's go – *'Yallah Shabaab'* – let's go friends.

FRENCH SLANG SAYINGS

'**BAC**' – French slang for police officer – an acronym for *'Brigade anti-criminalite'*. Also referred to as *'Flic'* – *'Hendek'* – *'Keuf'* – *'Poulet'* – *'Shtar'*.

'**Je me Casse**' – I am breaking up – I'm out of here – I'm leaving. (The title of the song from Malta in the 2021 Eurovision Contest by the singer *'Destiny'*).

A GERMAN SAYING

'Bulle' – German for *'bull'* – a slang word for police officer.

SAYINGS FROM INDIA
(With thanks to Ramesh Kumar Sharma)

'Achcha' – good.

'Arre' – hey!

'Baap re Baap' – Oh Father, Father.

'Baba Ji Ka Thulla' – absolutely nothing.

'Backchod' – liar.

'Bak bak' – *'chattering'* – talking a lot.

'Bakwaas' – nonsense.

'Bas' – that's it.

'Bindaas' – *'cool'* – exciting.

'Chakkar' – dizziness.

'Chalega' – that will do.

'Dhinchak' – *'bling'* – *'flashy'* – *'tacky'* – cheap-looking.

'Every two miles the water changes – every four miles the speech' – refers to the fact that in India there are 122 major languages and 1,599 minor spoken languages.

'Faadu' – amazing or outstanding.

'Fattu' – a *'wimp'* or weak person.

'Fuddu' – idiotic.

'Ghanta' – expresses disbelief.

'Hawabaazi' – show-off.

'Jhakaas' – fantastic.

'Jhand' – shattered or destroyed.

'Ji' – a suffix to show respect.

'Jugaad' – a solution.

'Mast' – awesome.

'Oye' – hey.

'Pakau' – very annoying person.

'Pakka' – sure.

'Pataka' – attractive lady.

'Thik Hain' – okay.

'Third Degree' – use of force – often relating to the police – long and harsh or coercive questioning by the police to obtain information or a confession.

'Vella' – lazy person.

'Waat Lag Gayi' – you are in serious trouble.

'Yaar' – friend.

IRANIAN SAYINGS IN FARSI
(With thanks to Majid Saili and Zohreh Dalton)

'Avizun' – hanging onto something or someone.

'Baba Joon' – a term of endearment.

'Dahan servis kardan' – really annoying.

'Jabroni' or *'mook'* – a silly, or foolish person.

'Kerm rikhtan' – to play someone up.

'Pichundan' – to avoid meeting or doing something.

'*Sar-e kar gozashtan*' – to tease someone.

'*Seh soot*' – instantly.

'*Sooti*' – make a mistake.

'*Tablo*' – clear picture – something obvious.

'*Tikeh andakhtan*' – sarcastic.

SOME SAYINGS FROM THE PHILIPPINES
(With thanks to Elma Bacani-Christou)

'*Basta*' – enough!

'*Charot*' – '*just kidding*'.

'*Chibog*' – food or eating time.

'*Gigil*' – feeling overwhelmed.

'*Kilig*' – '*butterflies in the stomach*' – nervous feeling.

'*Lodi*' – idolise.

'*Nyek*' – '*oops*' – surprised or shocked.

'*Susmariosep*' – receiving shocking news.

POLISH SAYINGS

'*An old Miss*' – married.

'*An old man*' – married man.

'*Bobo*' – stupid.

'*Nara*' – '*bye for now*' – '*see ya*' – informal goodbye.

'*Zajebiscie*' – awesome.

PORTUGUESE SAYINGS

'Bofia' – derogatory term for police and law enforcement.

'Bread is bread and cheese is cheese' – it is simple.

'Os Lobos' – the *'wolves'* – the national rugby team of Portugal.

SPANISH SAYINGS

'Esta Piripi' – *'typsy'* – under the influence of alcohol.

'Mucha mierda' – *'break a leg'* – good luck.

'Vamos' – adapted to *'vamoose'* in English – go quickly.

TURKISH SAYINGS
(With thanks to Nesrin Ozkan)

'Aynasiz' – meaning *'those without a mirror'* – people who refuse to look closely at themselves and the results of their own actions – *'ayna'* for short.

'Become an ear-ring to the ear' – to learn a lesson.

'Broad beans won't get wet in one's mouth' – the person who cannot keep secrets.

'Collecting horseshoe' – becoming unsuccessful, falling behind, *'eating someone's dust.'*

'Effected by the evil eye' – being cursed – to get bad luck.

'Fall off from someone's eye' – *'fall from favour'* – being disgraced.

'Flash like a straw fire' – to flare up too quickly.

'Good health to your hands' – that was a nice meal.

'Lift someone up to the sky' – talk very highly of someone.

'Like falling off the roof' – *'out of the blue'* – unexpected.

'Partridge in the bag' – a job that is easy – *'a doddle'*.

'Pocket with a hole in it' – a person who cannot keep money – a *'big spender'*.

'To cut the branch that you are sitting on' – to *'cut off your nose to spite your face'* – *'shoot one's-self in the foot'* – to damage yourself by your actions.

'To get a worm inside' – feel suspicious or *'to smell a rat'*.

'To hunt flies' – stand idle, have no customers.

'To lay flour on a rope' – to lead someone a *'song and a dance'* – to make many excuses not to do a job.

'To leave a door open' – to allow a chance to go back or change your mind about something.

'To tell a fairy-tale' – *'spin a yarn'* – *'tell a cock and bull story'* – total fantasy.

'To throw something to the wilderness' – to underestimate – *'to brush aside'*.

'Tongue as big as a shoe' – someone who answers back in a rude manner.

'Tread on your vein' – to seize someone about a subject that is a *'bugbear'* or irritates them.

SAYINGS FROM ZIMBABWE
(With thanks to Dorothy Mutsvanemoto)

'A good knobkerrie is cut from far away places' – the follies of people who are new at a place are not known – the faults of those within the vicinity are more visible than those from afar.

'Another man's wound should not be laughed at' – do not mock those that are facing hardship because the same thing may happen to you.

'Makomborereo anowanzowira kune vanhu vasingakwanise kuashandisa' – literal – *'squashes fall or ripen where there are no pots'* – certain blessings, talents or fortune seem to follow those who are least capable of utilising such good fortune.

'She respects even the family to which she is not betrothed' – one must respect all people, particularly their elders, and not just ones you are related to.

'That which has horns cannot be hidden in a sack' – some evil deeds cannot be hidden for ever as they have a way of being revealed.

'What men fail to handle should be reported' – one should give voice to their distress so that they can be helped.

15

UK MILITARY SAYINGS

ARMY

*(With thanks to Andy Woollaston and
Brian Preece – both former Coldstream Guards)*

'All in stew' – normally food served whilst on the ranges. An *'all in stew'* consisted of *'leftovers'* of what was not eaten at breakfast or dinner which would be in the container for tea.

'Award' – you can receive an *'award'* in the Army for doing something good i.e. a sports prize, and for doing something bad i.e. dirty boots which for example you could be given a Company Commander *'award'* with a fine of £60 or five days restrictions of privileges.

'Bad or Rag Order' – you're said to have been in *'bad or rag order'* if your kit, uniform, yourself or your vehicle is dirty or untidy, or the Inspecting person has *'got out of the wrong side of the bed'*.

'Baggage fatigue duties' – normally once a year the Royal Family go to Balmoral for a break from Royal duties. If assigned to *'baggage duties'* a detachment of Guardsmen and Non-Commissioned officers with a number of 4-ton trucks go to Buckingham Palace to collect and load the trucks with the Royals' belongings including pots and pans. Following the loading of the vehicles the detachment is shown to a room in the Palace where they are treated to a bottle of *'Manns'* ale and cucumber sandwiches.

'Beasted' – discipline or punishment marching, normally 120 paces to the minute, the speed that the Light Infantry, Royal Green Jackets, and the Gurkha's march at normally.

'Blue red blue blood' – (Guards) Household Divisions Brigade of Guards colours said to have been taken from the Battle of Waterloo campaign medal ribbon, smart person of the Household Division, someone who will do well in the Guards, someone who is a keen Guardsman is said to have Blue Red Blue blood – *'BRB'*.

'BER'ed' – beyond economical repair, it's destroyed or would cost too much to repair, it would have to be replaced, it has been written off.

'BLR'ed' – beyond local repair, something that must be sent away for repair, cannot be repaired in-house.

'Bolo' – someone who marches with a roll, cocky or with a swagger in their action, wears military uniform normally headgear in a *'Bolo'* fashion cocked to one side.

'Buckshee' – something free, spare, or surplus kit which you are not allowed to have in the military.

'Casevac' – something no-one wants to hear on the radio – casualty evacuation.

'Chinned Strapped' – very tired through lack of sleep.

'Chitty' – form.

'CORGI' – Commanding Officers really good idea.

'COY' – Company.

'Dhobi' – to do your *'dhobi'* is to do your laundry or submit it to stores for them to arrange for it to be done.

'Doss Bag' – sleeping bag.

'Dream Factory' – Royal Military Academy Sandhurst.

'Egyptian PT' – meaning to go to sleep. It described the way in which arms were folded across the chest. Occurred when you sneaked off for a cheeky sports afternoon nap.

'Endex' – end of exercise, back to camp, shower and a beer.

'GEN' – what's the true gossip.

'GL' – *'Gleaming'* – in the Guards if you are *'gleaming'* you are good at something.

'Gutter Sniper' – a Guards term for Royal event street lining. Normally service personnel lining the streets at arm's length away from each other to stop the public moving forward towards the member of the Royal household or other dignitary they are protecting.

'Head Shed' – Commanding Officer.

'Inter Regiment' – Nicknames:

Household Cavalry – **'Donkey Wallopers'**.

Grenadier Guards – the **'gobblers'** because they *'run around like headless turkeys'*.

Coldstream Guards – the **'sheep shaggers'** because of something alleged to have happened on Wimbledon Common many, many years ago and **'Lilly Whites'** due to the white band around their forage cap.

Scots Guards – **'Jock Guards'** or the **'kiddies'**. In the 1600s they were the youngest of the three Guards Regiments at the time.

Irish Guards – **'Mick Guards'**.

'KFS' – Knife, Fork, and Spoon.

'Kits and Capes duties' – A Guards saying. If assigned to this duty you travel ahead of the Guard that will be mounted at one of the Royal Palaces in a 4-ton truck along with the other soldiers suitcases which contain their change of clothing from ceremonial uniform, plus personal hygiene and kit cleaning items. In the event of wet weather, you hand the Guardsmen their grey capes to protect their uniforms.

'Nose Bag' – haversack rations, food in a paper bag, sandwiches fruit etc.

'Old Sweat' – Veteran service person or someone who has some time in service.

'On Stag' – Guard duty, sentry duty, your tour of duty.

'Recce' – carry out reconnaissance of an area.

'Restriction of privileges' – a detailed insight from Andy Woollaston – *One of the punishments that the military can award is restriction of privileges, a typical punishment which could consist of the following – up at 6am and report to the Guardroom. Breakfast and report to the Cookhouse to clean the Battalion's pots and pans after breakfast, followed by potato peeling for dinner, and return to normal duties. Dinner time report to the Cookhouse and clean the Battalion's pots and pans after dinner, prepare potatoes for the evening meal before returning to normal duties. After evening meal clean the Battalion's pots and pans, then the remainder of the evening prepare your best uniform for the defaulter's parade at 2200 hours at the Guardroom where you will be inspected by the Duty Piquet officer. They will scrutinize every part of you and your uniform and if they find anything wrong you are back on orders the next day and extra restrictions could be awarded. If all is fine the process starts the same the next day until you have worked off your awarded restrictions. If your restriction happens to run into a weekend, on the Saturday and Sunday in the* afternoon you are given some exercise with the prisoners from the Guardroom, and then it will be decided at a moment's notice what order of dress you are in. It could be home service clothing, Scarlet tunic and bearskin, combats camouflage uniform, No. 2 dress like the old-style police uniform, or clean fatigues which could be overalls. You then get inspected for which you could gain further restrictions. You then put on full battle webbing and backpack which may be packed with normal battle equipment, sand, or bricks. You are then marched on the Drill Square and 'beasted' for at least thirty minutes to an hour, marching at 120 paces to the minute. Once you are on 'restrictions' it is hard to get off them. I have known someone who got a further seven days 'restrictions'. On his final night's inspection, the Piquet officer passed the Guardsman off as being in good order. The officer walked away and then returned to the Guardsman and asked him to lift his left boot up, which he did. The next thing heard was, 'Take his name Sergeant in Waiting – this man has a boot stud missing.' On speaking to the officer after the parade he stated that when the Guardsman was called to attention at the start of the parade, he noticed a stud fall from his boot.

'RTU'ed' – failed the course and returned to Unit.

'Rupert' – or *'chicko'* – a Guards saying – a young Commissioned officer straight from the *'dream factory'*.

'Scoff' – food.

'Skid lid' – steel helmet.

'Slop Jockey' – a military chef.

'Square bashing' – Drill practice.

'Swabbing' – cleaning – this could be the floors, cleaning the toilets, washroom or your own bed space – no-one leaves until the *'swabbing'* has been done.

'Take their name/lost their name/put on a fizzer' – do something wrong and you've lost your name for which you could be put before the Company Commander or on Commanding Officers Orders who would issue a punishment.

'Thunder Box' – field toilet.

'Very Nulli' – a Coldstream Guards phrase only – if you are very smart, well turned out or know a lot about your Regiment you are said to be *'very Nulli'* taken from the Regimental motto *'Nulli Secundus'* – *'Second to None'*.

(With thanks to Gillian Taylor former 'WRAC' – Women's Royal Army Corps Signals)

'Cheap as a NAAFI watch' – cheap.

'Chuffed to NAAFI breaks' – really pleased about something.

'Cookhouse' – canteen.

'Dhobi Dust' – washing powder.

'Doss bag' – sleeping bag.

'Egg Banjo' – egg *'sarnie'* – sandwich.

'Full Jack' – full Corporal.

'Groundsheet' – women of *'easy virtue'*.

'Lance Jack' – Lance Corporal

'Nato-style' – tea.

'Plankies' – Guardsmen.

'Shreddies' – men's underpants.

'Slack Jennies' – Wrens.

'**Swan Vestas**' – Military Police.

'**Works Parade**' – uniform inspection prior to starting work.

(With thanks to Ryan H Burrell)

'**Ally**' – someone looking *'cool'* in their equipment – usually battlefield dress.

'**Badmin**' – a person with bad administrative skills or poor organisational skills.

'**Bite**' – to get someone on a *'bite'* – to *'kid'* someone.

'**Bone**' – someone who is stupid.

'**Chad**' – rubbish.

'**Civi**' – civilian – someone not in the Armed Forces.

'**Common Dog**' – common sense.

'**Crap Hat**' – a derogatory term used by the Parachute Regiment to describe any other Regiments apart from themselves.

'**Crow**' – derogatory term originating from WWI – refers to the newest recruits in a Regiment.

'**Daysack**' – small backpack big enough to pack essentials for a short period.

'**Devil Dodger**' – Padre.

'**Drip**' – to moan about something or someone.

'**Flash**' – to lose your temper.

'**Foofoo powder**' – foot powder.

'**Gash**' – waste.

'**Gopping**' – disgusting.

'Green Time Machine' – sleeping bag.

'Hanging Out' – very tired.

'Hoofing' – of good quality.

'Honking' – dirty or horrible.

'Icers' – very cold.

'In your own time' – you are not going anywhere until it's done.

'Jack' – *'workshy'* person – does *'jacks**t'* – does nothing.

'Marking Time' – an unpleasant drill movement marching up and down *'on the spot'*. Can also mean *'career going nowhere'*.

'Minging' – drunk or horrible.

'Mucker' – good mate.

'Nutty' – sweets or chocolate.

'Ping' – volunteer someone.

'Proffers' – a long-term loan of an item from the stores using dubious means.

'Pull up a sandbag' – to tell a story.

'Queens' – the truth must be told.

'Redders' – really hot – *'red pigs'*.

'Run ashore' – a night out *'on the town'*.

'Scale a Parade' – a parade or gathering where every person attends with no excuses.

'Sippers' – share a drink.

'TAB' – Tactical Advance to Battle – Forced march.

'Threaders' – not happy.

'Turbo' – the very best.

'Walt' – *'Walter Mitty'* – fantasist.

'Waz' – brilliant.

'Wrap' – give up.

ROYAL AIR FORCE
(With thanks to Tony 'Bunny' Everett and Alan Taylor)

'Ack Ack' – anti-aircraft fire from the ground.

'AFC' – Air Force Cross.

'AG' – Air Gunner.

'Apron' – area for parking aircraft.

'Archie' – World War I name for anti-aircraft fire.

'ATC' – Air Training Corps.

'Bale' – *'bale out'* – leave the plane.

'Bang Out' – use ejection seat.

'BD' – Bomb Disposal.

'Beam' (on the) – right direction from radar beam.

'Beat Up' – fly low and fast over an area.

'Belly Land' – to land without wheels or an undercarriage.

'Binders' – aircraft brakes.

'Black Box' – any piece of electronic equipment – the 'flight recorder' boxes are orange.

'Blister' – a cockpit cover, or a written charge of some offence.

'Blitz' – to carry something out with a sense of speed or urgency.

'Blood Wagon' – ambulance.

'Blower' – supercharger on an aero engine, or a telephone.

'Bluebird' – a female RAF member or WAAF.

'Bogy' – enemy or unidentifiable aircraft.

'Bowser' – aircraft refuelling lorry – the name of the manufacturer.

'Bought It' – died.

'Char' – tea.

'Char and Wad' – tea and sandwiches.

'Chocks Away' – to remove safety chocks from aircraft wheels – or to leave a place.

'Circuits and Bumps' – aircraft landing and taking off immediately – usually a training exercise and sometimes called a *'roller'*.

'Chaddy' – untidy.

'Conkout' – to die, or an engine failure.

'Clampers' – airfield fog, very poor visibility.

'CPSU' – Carrier Pigeon Service Unit.

'Crackup' – to have an aircraft accident.

'Crump Dump' – bomb store.

'Daisy Cutter' – landing on grass.

'Dead Stick' – aircraft loses all power, engine failure.

'DFC' – Distinguished Flying Cross.

'Ditch' – crash or emergency landing on water.

'Drone' – a lesser person or a target towed behind an aircraft.

'Duff' – incorrect – *'duff gen'* – wrong information.

'Eggs' – bombs.

'Erk' – lower rank or new-recruits.

'Egg White' – Egypt.

'Fan' – propellor.

'Fizzer' – a written charge of alleged misconduct.

'Flack' – anti-aircraft fire or fall-out from an argument.

'Flap' – a time of disarray or panic – something requires urgent attention.

'FAA' – Fleet Air Arm.

'Flip' – a short aircraft journey or a *'joyride'*.

'Fruit Salad' – the rank markings on a senior officer's headwear.

'Full Bore' – maximum effort – engine on high power.

'Gen' – information, written or verbal.

'Gone for a Burton' – dead or killed – time to get your best suit out! Originates from RAF slang during the Second World War – an air gunners' phrase for being *'Killed in Action'*.

'Goon' – guard in a POW *'Prisoner of War'* camp.

'Gremlin' – a hard to find fault on an aircraft.

'HSL' – High Speed Launch.

'IANS' – Initial Air Navigation School.

'Jankers' – a punishment duty imposed by a senior officer, usually for a minor offence.

'Jink' – to avoid something or somebody. A manoeuvre carried out by an aircraft to avoid an enemy aircraft.

'Lineshoot' – a lie or an exaggerated story.

'Meatwagon' – the same as *'blood wagon'* – an ambulance.

'Mega' – big or large.

'N' – infinite, forever.

'Old Newton' – gravity – an aircraft's enemy.

'Pongo' – other military services – referring to a soldier in the Army.

'Prang' – accident – usually relating to an aircraft.

'Pukka' – real or genuine e.g. *'Pukka Gen'* – good information.

'QCS' – Queens Colour Squadron.

'QHI' – Qualified Helicopter Instructor.

'RAFC' – Royal Air Force College.

'SACW' – Senior Aircraft-woman.

'Scramble' – aircraft taking off for a military objective.

'Shiney' – a military person who's trade or profession does not involve working with aircraft – they sit in offices *'shining'* the seat of the chair.

'SMO' – Senior Medical Officer.

'SP' – Staging Post.

'Sprog' – a recruit.

'Sparkie' – *'sparks'* – a tradesman or woman whose trade involved electricity or radio.

'Taters' – cold.

'Through the Gate' – to push an engine beyond its normal high-power setting.

'VAD' – Voluntary Aid Detachment.

'WAAF' – Women's Auxiliary Air Force.

'Wad' – sandwich.

'Walla' – man e.g. *'wheel walla'* – driver or *'rivet walla'* – airframe mechanic.

'Yonks' – long period of time.

'Zulu' – local time.

ROYAL NAVY
(With thanks to Richard Jones)

'AB' – Able Seaman.

'Adrift' – to be late.

'Andrew – The' – the Royal Navy – said to have originated from the *'press gang'* leader Andrew Miller.

'Babies Heads' – tinned steak and kidney pie.

'Bimble' – walk slowly – *'bimble along'*.

'Bish' – the Naval Chaplain.

'BZ' – a naval term – a combination of *'Bravo'* and *'Zulu'* – meaning 'well done' sent either by nautical flags, by flag hoist or radio signal, in relation to actions, operations or performance.

'Chop one off' – salute.

'Civvy Street' – civilian life.

'CO' – Commanding Officer.

'CPO' – Chief Petty Officer.

'Crabfat' – a member of the RAF.

'Crusher' – member of the Royal Navy Police *(RNP)* or the Regulating Petty Officer in charge of administration and discipline – *'Reggie'*.

'Dhobie' – wash.

'Dose' – sexually transmitted disease.

'Exped' – Adventurous training.

'Fair winds and calm seas' – a gesture of good luck to those who have served with honour and courage – a naval farewell – a toast of salutation between Mariners.

'Fighting Irons' – knife, fork and spoon.

'Galley' – kitchen.

'Goat Locker' – an area on board a naval vessel reserved for the exclusive use of Chief Petty Officers. Said to originate from the time when ships were wooden and *'CPOs'* oversaw looking after the goat's milk on board.

'Glamour Spanner' – hair comb.

'Grey Funnel Line' – Royal Navy.

'Heads' – the ships toilets.

'Ickies' – foreign currency.

'Jackspeak' – slang words used by the *'Senior Service'*.

'Jenny' – a Wren – female sailor.

'Jolly' – stopover on shore leave.

'Kit Muster' – personal kit inspection.

'Lingo' – local language.

'Loafing' – being idle – *'hanging around'* not doing much.

'Matelot' – British sailor.

'MID' – Mentioned in Despatches.

'NAAFI' – Navy, Army and Air Force Institute – a place to buy goods and foodstuff.

'NATO standard' – tea or coffee with milk and two sugars.

'Notice of call-out for Service' – Royal Fleet Reserve – a notice exercised under powers pursuant to Section 26 of the Reserves Forces Act 1980 to be called back for permanent service.

'Oggin' – at sea or in the water.

'Oppo' – mate or *'buddy'*.

'Percy' – a soldier – *'pongo'*.

'Pipe' – announcement over main broadcast.

'Quaff' – to drink.

'Rack' – bunk, bed, or *'shelf'*.

'Rat-arsed' – drunk.

'Royal' – Royal Marine or *'Bootneck'*.

'Shippers' – shipmate.

'Sʷ*ʷtehawk'** – seagull.

'Scran' – food.

'Side' – bosun's whistle – salute to Lord High Admiral – about to come *'on board'*.

'Sippers' – a sip from a drink – normally rum – as opposed to *'gulpers'* – taking a large mouthful.

'Spinning a Dit' – telling a story – usually in a light-hearted manner.

'Sprog (2)' – someone who has only been in the Navy for a short time.

'Still' – bosun's whistle – *'stand where you are'*.

'Tot' – a measure of rum.

'Turn to' – start work.

'Wafu' – a member of the Fleet Air Arm.

'Wardroom' – officers mess.

'Wet' – taking a drink – usually tea.

'Yellow Peril' – kippers/smoked haddock – a phrase more common among submariners.

'Zeds' – sleep.

UK POLICE FORCES
MISCELLANEOUS SAYINGS

Reference book *'One in for D&D'* available on Amazon.co.uk for West Midlands Police sayings.

'ASAP' – As Soon As Possible – *'A-sap'* – *'on the hurry up'* – *'grade one shout'* – *'immediate response'*.

'A shout' – *'a job'* – an incident or call resulting in a resource being despatched often by police radio.

'As straight as a die' – totally honest.

'As bent as a nine-bob note' – totally dishonest.

'ARV' – Armed Response Vehicle.

'Bang Out of Order' – doing something very wrong.

'Bang to Rights' – having enough evidence to accuse them of committing a crime – *'over a barrel'*.

'Battenburg' – reflective markings on police vehicles in yellow/blue squares.

'Batting for England' – trying to shift responsibility for doing something as far away as possible from themselves.

'Blues and Twos' – emergency flashing blue lights and two-frequency sirens.

'Brief' – solicitor.

'Call Sign' – the name or numbers allocated to a resource and normally used on the radio in preference to the use of an officer's name, rank or *'collar number'*.

'Carry on' – *'as you were'* – go back to what you were doing.

'CHIS' – Covert Human Intelligence Source – *'snout'* – *'sarbut'* – *'coppers narc'* – informant.

'Couldn't organise a piss up in a brewery' – disorganised – no proper planning.

'Clear' – a phrase often associated with searching premises to indicate that a room is empty or no threats to safety are apparent.

'Cuckooing' – the illegal practice of taking over a person's residence to use it for criminal activities such as the supply of controlled drugs.

'DOB' – Date of Birth.

'D's' – Detectives.

'Do One!' – depart with a sense of urgency! – do a disappearing act! Usually reserved for someone who is behaving in an anti-social manner and on their last warning prior to arrest. Northern English and used frequently in the Liverpool series *'Brookside'* in the 1990s.

'Do your thirty' – complete thirty years pensionable police service – *'got your time in'.*

'Early doors' – the time to execute search warrants – early hours of the morning – earlier than usual.

'Easy touch' – gullible – easily taken in by someone.

'ETA' – estimated time of arrival.

'Fessed Up' – confessed.

'Fit Up' – a fabrication of evidence.

'Fixer' – a criminal who sorts out problems for other criminals.

'FR' – further report or update on a crime report or incident.

'Given a pull' – subjected to a stop and search.

'Guvnor' – 'Boss' – 'Ma'am' – 'Gaffer' – senior officer of Inspector or above in rank.

'Hasn't got a leg to stand on' – no excuse – no defence – excuses won't hold up.

'Heads Up' – make somewhere aware of something.

'Hobby Bobby' – a historical term of a derogatory nature referring to Special Constables.

'Iffy' – 'sus' – suspicious or strange.

'IC 1' – white male.

'In the frame' – suspected of being involved in something.

'Job' – the police.

'Juliet' – the phonetic letter of the alphabet for 'J'.

'Kicked off' – disturbance.

'Legged it' – run off.

'Leak' – unlawful disclosure of information.

'MOE' – method of entry.

'MOP' – Member of the public.

'NABIS' – National Ballistics Intelligence Service.

'Nick' – police station.

'Nicked' – 'collar *felt*' – arrested.

'No Comment' – when a suspect declines to provide an answer to a question whilst *'under caution'* during police questioning.

'N/T' – no trace.

'OCG' – Organised Crime Group.

'On the straight and narrow' – on best behaviour – avoiding getting into trouble.

'OSMAN Warning' – a warning of a death threat or risk of murder issued by the police or authorities to the prospective victim based on a 'duty of care'.

'OT' – overtime.

'Plan B' – what to do when *'Plan A'* fails – *'if all else fails'*.

'Playing his or her face' – describing someone being *'mouthy'* or disorderly.

'POLAC' – accident involving a police vehicle.

'Plus TA' – time of arrival at the scene of an incident to be added to the log.

'PNC' – Police National Computer.

'Pro-Con' – *'probie'* – *'sprog'* – probationer constable with under two years' service.

'Put your ticket in' – resign or retire.

'Q' word' – a reference to never using the phrase 'it's quiet' during a police shift as it is usually seen as a bad luck omen and a precursor to suddenly becoming busy.

'Run like the clappers' – run at high-speed. Usually referring to a suspect who managed to escape arrest. *'Clappers'* are things inside church-bells which make a ringing sound. A vigorously rung bell implied a sense of urgency or speed.

'RV' – stipulated rendezvous point.

'Scroat' – criminal – *'CRO'* – someone with a criminal record.

'Scuffler' – football hooligan or someone who likes to fight.

'Shifting a bit' – speeding, *'getting a move on'*, going fast.

'Sit Rep' – situation update on a report of an incident.

'Snap' – meal break.

'Snow Dropper' – someone who steals clothing from washing lines.

'Snowed under' – over-worked.

'So far' – sending a partial message via the radio and seeking confirmation of receipt – *'yes-yes'* – confirmation of receipt or *'roger'*.

'Spin a drum' – search a house.

'Spinning' – the *'art'* of causing someone to turn around quickly by some act of subterfuge and then to deny all knowledge of any such act. Usually done to 'amuse' others present.

'Spliff' – cannabis – *'blow'* – *'joint'* – *'herbal'* – *'hashish'* – *'black'* – *'reefer'*.

'Springer' – someone who habitually buys the drinks in a pub.

'Squealer' – someone who has provided information to the police – *'grass'*.

'Squirrelled away' – hidden or stored in a safe place.

'Stand By' – *'wait one'* – wait for a further radio transmission.

'TADA' – take and drive away a motor vehicle.

'TAG' – the unique *'signature'* of a so-called *'graffiti artist'* on a piece of graffiti.

'The Big House' – Crown Court.

'Thin blue line' – the barrier between civilized society and chaos.

'TK' – phone box.

'Torched' – set on fire – usually referred to in a case of arson.

'TSG' – Territorial Support Group – public order trained officers.

'Up to scratch' – meets the standard – come up to proof.

'Up to your eyeballs in it' – heavily involved in the context of committing a crime.

'USGs' – Urban Street Gangs.

'VO' – Visiting Order to see prisoners in HM Prisons.

'Whisky' – phonetic alphabet for letter 'W'.

'X-Ray' – phonetic alphabet letter for 'X'.

'Yankee' – phonetic alphabet letter for 'Y'.

'Zulu' – the last letter in the phonetic alphabet used by the police to spell out letters or words.

BRITISH TRANSPORT POLICE SAYINGS

Visit the British Transport Police History Group website for other sayings and special thanks to Philip Trendall.

'BONGO' – *'Books On Never Goes Out'* – *'Olympic Torch'*.

'BTP' – British Transport Police.

'CFW' – a concern for welfare call on the radio to ensure that a member of the public, an officer or member of staff is ok.

'Cough' – an admission to an offence made by a suspect.

'Dip' – a professional pickpocket usually found on the London Underground. At one stage a dedicated team of officers known as the *'Dip Squad'* was set up by BTP on the *'LU'* to tackle organised gangs many of whom travelled to the UK from other countries and were highly organised.

'Double back' – a *'quick change around'* – where there was a gap of just eight hours between the end of one shift and the start of another.

'Flasher' – Indecent exposure by males on women.

'Gurkha' – an officer with a reputation for not taking prisoners.

'In the Bin' – a person in custody or *'PIC'*.

'MICC' – *'Management Information & Communications Centre'* *'FHQ'* – Force Headquarters.

'Moles' – officers who worked full-time on London Underground.

'OB' – Occurrence Book.

'On the Cushions' – travelling by train to escort back football supporters who were somewhere in the country at an 'away game' – usually a group or numbers who had not been expected to travel. A *'scratch'* serial of officers would be put together to travel up in the afternoon of a match day to be at the place of departure in time for after the game finished. The reference related to being able to sit down in a carriage on the way there.

'One Under' – A reference to a fatality on the railway. It usually relates to someone being hit by a train and the fact that the body is often found underneath a carriage.

'OSU' – Operations Support Unit – public order trained officers.

'Pavement Artist' – a criminal who specialised in armed robbery.

'RAIL' – Command and Control system – *'Resource Allocation & Incident Logging'*.

'Red Devil/Red Peril' – Arrest reports which were completed in triplicate with the actual forms being red in colour.

'SB' – Special Branch – historically related to CID officers but in more recent times to those officers dedicated to aspects of counter-terrorism work.

'The Dairy' – FHQ at the old Tavistock Place in London which was the former HQ of Express Dairies.

'The Rattler' – London Underground train.

'T.I – S (5) (3) (a)' – Ticket Irregularity – Section 5 (3) (a) Regulation of Railways Act 1889 – if any person travels, or attempts to travel on a railway without having previously paid their fare, and with intent to avoid payment thereof shall be guilty of an offence. Some of the evidential aspects to prove such an offence include failing to produce a ticket on request, failing to pay their fare from the place where the journey started or failing to provide their name and address – known as the *'three fails'*.

'TMB' – Telephone Message Book.

'Van Dragging' – police tactic following British Rail delivery drivers to catch either *'jump up'* thieves who would enter the lorries/vans whilst they were left unattended during deliveries or drivers who were themselves involved in parcel theft.

18

POST OFFICE INVESTIGATION BRANCH SAYINGS

(With thanks to Harry Wynne)

'BRUTE' – *'British Rail Universal Trolley Equipment'* – used to convey GPO mailbags on railway stations – usually a series of wired cages on wheels pulled along at the front by a small tractor.

'Chummy' – the suspect under investigation.

'Gallery' – an overhead passageway in a GPO Sorting Office just wide enough for a person to stand in to be able to observe staff members suspected of committing thefts via *'one-way glass'*.

'Take someone on' – watch an employee on their *'rounds'* who was suspected of stealing parcels or letters.

'The thieves itch' – whilst observing staff members who were suspected of stealing letters or parcels the investigators noticed a pattern of behaviour whereby a suspect who appeared to be trying to come to a decision as to whether to steal something or not would start scratching either behind their ear or their backside – clearly a sign of nerves *'kicking in'*.

'TPOs' – *'Travelling Post Offices'* – trains carrying the mail.

19

HER MAJESTY'S PRISONS SLANG

(With thanks to Jag Mavi)

'App' – application to the Governor.

'Association' – a time limited period of mixing with other prisoners.

'Banged up' – locked in a cell – in prison – *'in the jug'*.

'Baron' – an old-fashioned term for a prisoner with influence on a prison wing who would, among other things, run the *'black market'* when tobacco – *'snout'* – was the currency in use to exercise control and gain financially or through favours owed.

'Block' – solitary confinement – punishment wing.

'Boss' – the term used by prisoners to address prison officers.

'Cards Marked' – done something that is disapproved of by someone in authority.

'Cell spin' – cell search by prison staff.

'Clink' – *'chokey'* – prison.

'Doing bird' – *'doing time'* – serving a prison sentence.

'First night cell' – the cell used by a newly arrived prisoner at Prison on their first night of incarceration.

'Ghosted' – moved to another prison.

'Grass' – *'squealer'* – *'rat'* – *'narc'* – *'snitch'* – informant.

'HMP' – Her Majesty's Prison.

'Induction' – the first few days of prison life learning *'the ropes'* and the prison system.

'Lag' – inmate or prisoner – 'old lag' – long serving prisoner.

'Landing' – the area immediately outside a cell area.

'Lifer' – prisoner serving a life sentence.

'Meds' – prescribed medicine.

'Nick you' – put you on a discipline charge within prison.

'Nonce' – a person in prison for offences against children or a sex offender.

'Padmate' – cellmate.

'Peer Workers' – trusted prisoners – formally known as *'red bands'* who wore one on their arms.

'Porridge' – 'stir' – prison sentence.

'Release on Temporary Licence' – short period of release from prison for such things as going for job interviews or family visits on welfare grounds.

'Rub down' – the search of a prisoner.

'Screw' – *'kanga'* – prison officer.

'Seg' – segregation wing or area.

'Shank' – improvised stabbing weapon.

'Slop Out' – the practice of emptying a bucket of urine and human waste into a toilet before the introduction of toilets into cells.

'Snout' – cigarette – *'little fellahs'* – cigarette-ends – Northern saying.

'**Stash**' – a place where a prisoner's contraband is hidden or the actual items themselves.

'**Shtoom**' – keep quiet.

'**The Yard**' – exercise yard.

'**Top or bottom**' – a decision as to which bunk a prisoner takes.

'**VO**' – Visiting Order to see a prisoner – usually families, legal representatives, or police.

'**VP Wing**' – a wing for vulnerable prisoners.

'**What are you doing?**' – what sentence did you get?

20

HEALTH SLANG AND SAYINGS

'AAU' – Acute Admissions Unit – as in *'Holby City'*.

'A & E' – Accident and Emergency Department.

'Appy' – appendicitis.

'Baby Catcher' – obstetrician.

'Bloodsuckers' – someone who takes blood samples such as phlebotomists.

'BONITA' – *'Big Old Needle in The Ass'*.

'BP' – Blood Pressure.

'Chocolate hostage' – constipation.

'Code Brown' – clean up required for problems with diarrhoea.

'Code Yellow' – patient with loss of bladder control.

'COPD' – Chronic Obstruction Pulmonary Disease – a lung condition.

'Detox' – detoxification – the process of removing toxins from the body – usually associated with drugs or alcohol.

'Dicky Ticker' – heart problems.

'DOA' – Dead on arrival.

'ECU' – *'Eternal Care Unit'* – death.

'ERCP' – endoscopic retrograde cholangiopancreatography – procedure to diagnose and treat problems in the liver, gallbladder, bile ducts and pancreas.

'Fair to middlin' – not feeling 100% well.

'F.A.S.T.' – pneumonic for the possible symptoms of a stroke effecting the following and what the priority is – FACE – ARMS – SPEECH – TIME.

'Feeling under the weather' – poorly.

'Foley' – catheter used to drain bladder of urine.

'Frequent Flyer' – someone who attends hospital seeking attention for every little health problem.

'Freud Squad' – the psychiatry department.

'GP' – General Practitioner.

'Happy Juice' – a cocktail of medication given *'pre-op'* or to reduce pain.

'Hasselhoff' – bizarre injuries.

'IV Fluids' – Intravenous fluids – liquids given to replace water, sugar and salt you might need if ill or having an operation and can't drink as normal.

'Med School' – medical school.

'Nil by Mouth' – a common expression indicating that the patient will not be consuming food prior to undertaking an operation.

'Noctor' – a nurse who behaves like a doctor.

'NPS' – *'New Parent Syndrome'* – panicking new parents who take their children to hospital for every little problem.

'Off the clock' – not at work – off duty – not being paid for working.

'PAFO' – *'Pissed and Fell Over'* – being drunk and falling.

'Pick Up' – an ambulance service call to pick up a patient.

'PITA' – *'Pain in The Ass'* – an uncooperative patient or relative.

'PPE' – Personal Protective Equipment.

'Resus' – resuscitation.

'Rose Cottage' or *'Ivy Cottage'* – the hospital mortuary.

'Scrubs' – personal protection medical clothing.

'Sectioned' – committed compulsorily to a psychiatric facility in accordance with a section of the Mental Health Act.

'Shot gunning' – ordering a wide range of tests in the hope that one will show what's wrong with the patient.

'STI' – Sexually Transmitted Infection – in *'street slang'* referred to as a *'dose of the clap'* or more formally *'VD'* – venereal disease.

'Stream Team' – a team of urologists.

'TEETH' – *'Tried Everything Else – Try Homeopathy'*.

'The Wagon' – an ambulance.

'UTI' – Urinary Tract Infection.

'Vent Jockey' – respiratory therapist.

'You might just feel a small sharp prick' – the standard preface to having an injection.

'404 moment' – the moment in a doctor's ward rounds when a patient's medical records cannot be found.

21

SPORTING SAYINGS AND NICKNAMES

'Beat someone to the punch' – anticipate and react to a move or action.

'Below the belt' – an illegal punch in boxing – below the opponent's *'belt'*.

'Down to the wire' – result in question to the very end or last minute.

'Glass Jaw' – in boxing someone who is vulnerable to a knockout punch.

'Go the distance' – complete all the rounds in a boxing match.

'On the ropes' – on the verge of defeat in boxing.

'Par for the course' – only to be expected.

'Slam dunk' – a forceful or dramatic move in basketball.

'Sticky wicket' – a difficult pitch in cricket – damp or soft but drying out rapidly.

'Wemberley' – Wembley Stadium.

FOOTBALL CLUB NICKNAMES

'Addicks' – Charlton Athletic.

'Baggies' – West Bromwich Albion.

'Bees' – Brentford.

'Blackcats' – Sunderland.

'Blades' – Sheffield United.

'Bluebirds' – Cardiff City.

'Blues' – Birmingham City.

'Blues' – Chelsea – or *'The Pensioners'*.

'Canaries' – Norwich City.

'Carpetmen' – Kidderminster Harriers.

'Cherries' – Bournemouth.

'Choirboys' – Wycombe Wanderers.

'City' – Manchester City or *'the citizens'*.

'Clarets' – Burnley.

'Eagles' – Crystal Palace.

'Forest' – Nottingham Forest.

'Foxes' – Leicester City.

'Gunners' – Arsenal.

'Hammers' – West Ham.

'Hatters' – Luton Town.

'Hoops' – Queens Park Rangers.

'Hornets' – Watford.

'Lilywhites' – Preston North End.

'Lions' – Millwall.

'Magpies' – Newcastle.

'Millers' – Rotherham United.

'Monkey Hangers' – Hartlepool.

'**Owls**' – Sheffield Wednesday.

'**Peacocks**' – Leeds United.

'**Potters**' – Stoke City.

'**Rams**' – Derby County.

'**Red Devils**' – Manchester United.

'**Red Wall**' – Welsh national team.

'**Reds**' – Liverpool.

'**Robins**' – Bristol City.

'**Royals**' – Reading.

'**Saddlers**' – Walsall.

'**Saints**' – Southampton.

'**Seagulls**' – Brighton and Hove.

'**Shrimps**' – Morecambe.

'**Sky Blues**' – Coventry City.

'**Smoggies**' – Middlesbrough.

'**Swans**' – Swansea.

'**Terriers**' – Huddersfield Town.

'**Toffees**' – Everton.

'**Toons**' – Newcastle United.

'**Trotters**' – Bolton Wanderers.

'**Tykes**' – Barnsley.

'**Villa**' – Aston Villa.

'**Wolves**' – Wolverhampton Wanderers.

A FEW RUGBY CLUB NICKNAMES

'Dragons' – Wales national rugby team.

'Harlequins RFC' – play at Twickenham.

'Leicester Tigers' – Leicester RFC.

'Red Roses' – national women's team for England.

'Sale Sharks' – Sale RFC.

'The Lions' – the British & Irish Lions rugby union team selected from eligible players for the national teams of the *'Home Nations'* of England, Scotland, Wales, Northern Ireland and Ireland.

'The Wasps' – Coventry RFC.

'Worcester Warriors' – Worcester RFC.

22

CHOIR AND THEATRE SAYINGS

'Break A Leg' – good luck – it's bad luck to say *'good luck'* in the theatre.

'Like a fire in a pet shop' – a derogatory term to describe a display of very bad singing.

23

SCHOOL ABBREVIATIONS

'DfE' – Department for Education.

'DSL' – Designated Safeguarding Lead.

'EAL' – English as an additional language.

'PE' – Physical Education.

'PTA' – Parent Teacher Association.

'QTS' – Qualified Teacher Status.

'RE' – Religious Education.

'SATs' – Standard Assessment Tests.

'TA' – Teaching Assistant.

24

MONEY SAYINGS

'Ackers' – money. Believed to originate from the Egyptian word *'akka'* relating to a coin.

'Bangers and Mash' – Cockney slang for cash.

'Benjamins' – a hundred-dollar bill – originates from the face on the note which is that of Benjamin Franklin.

'Brass' – money.

'Bucks' – Dollars.

'Bullseye' – £50.

'Cheap as chips' – doesn't cost much.

'Costs a bomb' – very expensive.

'Cough up' – pay up.

'Filthy lucre' – money obtained dishonestly. Comes from the Bible where it refers to those who teach wrongly for the sake of money.

'Grand' – £1,000.

'Greens' – American banknotes which are green in colour.

'Loot' – money.

'Minted' – well-off – rich.

'Nicker' – A pound.

'Peppered' – a phrase used in Manchester for having no money.

'Pony' – £25 – originates from the days of the Raj in India when some Indian Rupee banknotes bore pictures of animals.

'Rip off' – not worth the cost.

'Score' – £20.

'Splashing out' – spending a lot.

'Tap someone up' – ask for money.

'Ten Bob Note' – ten-shilling note in old money. Now worth just 50 pence. Its origins go back to August 1914 when the economy was in turmoil and prior to the First World War the Government in the form of the Treasury took the unusual step of issuing the notes to enable the public to make small transactions. As part of the process of decimalisation the note was replaced in 1969 with the new fifty pence coin.

'Tight as a duck's arse' – thrifty.

'Ton' – £100.

'Quid' – a pound.

'Zilch' – penniless.

25

WEATHER SLANG

'Back end weather' – used in the East Midlands to indicate autumnal weather.

'Cloudburst' – heavy downpour.

'Close' – *'sticky'* – humid atmosphere.

'Coming down in stair rods' – heavy rain – used in the North of England.

'Cow Quaker' – rain so heavy that the cows shake.

'It's looking black over Bill's Mother's' – a phrase claimed by a number of areas in the UK. The Birmingham version is that *'Bill's Mother'* was the mother of William Shakespeare and that *'Brummies'* used to look towards Stratford-Upon-Avon and when there were dark clouds indicate with the phrase that a storm was coming. It's also the title of a historical crime fiction book in the *'Made in Birmingham'* series.

'Lashing it down' – heavy rain.

'Letting' – a term in Somerset for rain which is heavy enough to cause a problem.

'Never cast a clout until May be out' – a clout is an old word for a piece of clothing. The saying means don't take your warm clothes off until the May blossom is out because cold weather can return in the Spring months.

'Oak before Ash we'll just have a slash; ash before oak we're in for a soak' – if the oak leaves come before the ash we are set to have light rain over the summer but if the leaf buds of the ash burst through first then a soaking wet summer is guaranteed.

'Picking' – a Welsh term for rain starting.

'Pissing it down' – a steady stream of rain.

'Plothering' – a term for heavy rain in the Midlands and the North East.

'Raining cats and dogs' – heavy non-stop rain – originates from the 17th century.

'Raining Forks' – *'tiyunsdown'ards'* – a Lincolnshire phrase for raining like pitchforks.

'Red sky at night – shepherds delight' – fair weather headed your way.

'Smir' – a Scottish term for light rain.

'Spitting' – light rain – used in Manchester – also referred to as *'mizzling'* in Warwickshire.

'Sprinkle' or *'spot'* of rain – very little rain.

'Stoating' – heavy rain in Scotland that bounces off the ground.

'Z Time' – *'Zulu Time'* – twenty-four hour clock and Greenwich Mean Time zone used in weather forecasts that also have military connotations.

26

TOILET SLANG

'*A dose of the s**ts*' – diarrhoea.

'*Bobbar*' – a word used in Sheffield for faeces.

'*Caught short*' – needing to go to the toilet promptly.

'*Closet*' – toilet.

'*Drop the kids off at the pool*' – go to the toilet.

'*Gypsies kiss*' – '*piss*' – '*pee*' – urinate or '*pass water*'.

'*Jimmy Riddle*' – '*piddle*' – urinate.

'*Jobby*' – a Scottish term for a '*poo*' – faeces.

'*Kacked in his Pants*' – had a bowel movement in his underwear.

'*Lav*' – lavatory – toilet.

'*Little boy's room*' – '*gents*' – men's toilets.

'*Loo*' – toilet.

'*No 1*' – urinate.

'*No 2*' – defecate.

'*Pee*' – urinate.

'*Poop*' – defecate.

'*Privy*' – toilet.

'*Regular as clockwork*' – bowel movements at the same time each day.

'Slash' – urinate.

'Spurt' – urinate.

Squeeze your nose and pull the chain – using hand signs – going to the toilet.

'Swamp' – a term for urinating in the Army.

'Take a Dump' – empty your bowels.

'The Jacks' – a toilet in Ireland.

'The Runs' – diarrhoea.

'Tinkle' – urinate.

'The Bog' – toilet. The term goes back to 1789 and is short for *'boghouse'* and comes from the British slang *'to defecate'*.

'The Khazi' – toilet. Like the Cockney word *'carsey'* and widely used in Liverpool.

'The Loo' – toilet. Deriving from the French *'Guardez l'eau'* which means *'watch out for the water'*. The original English version was *'gardy-loo'* which then became shortened.

'The Trots' – a bout of diarrhoea.

'To have a crap' – defecate. A British Company called *'Thomas Crapper & Co Ltd.'* manufactured toilets in Britain. American soldiers later shortened the name to Crap.

'Thunderbox' – primitive outside toilet normally contained in a small wooden shed with a hole in the ground, in the bottom of which lime would be spread.

'Syphon the maggot' – go to the toilet.

ACKNOWLEDGEMENTS
AND REFERENCES

arkroyal.net

Elma Bacani-Christou

BBC Manchester

BBC Northern Ireland

BBC Weather

Anna Bigus

Cheryl Birbeck

birminghamhistory.co.uk

British Transport
Police History Group

Britishcouncil.org

Colin Bryan

Ryan H Burrell

Marios Christou

Niki Ioannou-Christou

Loukia Christou-Hawas

Cockneyrhymingslang.co.uk

collinsdictionary.com

Coventry Telegraph

ChangeChecker.Org

Chris

Joyce Cooke-Taylor

Barry Crowley

Culture Trip

Zohreh Dalton

Maggie Doyle

Tony *'Bunny'* Everett

David Faulkner

football-stadiums.co.uk

Forces.net

Funtrivia.com

Grace Hampson

Samir Hawas

Carol Heath

Caitlin – Highland Titles

i-Yorkshire.com

Richard Jones

Ramesh Kumar Sharma

Lakecountryhouse.co.uk

Nicki Layton

Sharon Layton

Bob Lessemun

Roger Lomas

manchestereveningnews.com

Paul Majster

Jag Mavi

John McBride

merriam-webster.com

Dorothy Mutsvanemoto

Susan Nicholls

northernirishman
inpoland.com

nursebuff.com

Nesrin Ozkan

Gary Padfield

Gordon Padfield

phrases.org.uk

plumbworld.co.uk

Brian Preece

Queensland.com

David Rischmiller

rnsubs.co.uk

Bill Rogerson

Janet Russell

Majid Saili

Scotsman.com

sedgleymanor.com

Lynn Selby

Anya Small

Richard Small

Smarty's Blog Bristolian
Dictionary

Stepfeed.com

Marion Steward

Alan Taylor

Gillian Taylor

theculturetrip.com

thefreedictionary.com

theguardian.com

timeanddate.com

Darryll Thomas

translationdirectory.com

Philip Trendall

urbandictionary.com

Amy Watkins

welearnwelsh.com

Wiktionary.org

Wikipedia

Nicola Wilson

Andy Woollaston

writingexplained.org

Harry Wynne

XeniaStudents.com

OTHER BOOKS BY MICHAEL LAYTON
AND STEPHEN BURROWS

Joint:

Historical Crime Fiction:

Black Over Bill's Mother's – A Storm is Coming

Pretty Thing (S. Burrows)

Keep Right On

The Touch of Innocence

Non-Fiction:

One in For D & D – a little book of police slang

It's A Blag – police tricks and funny stories

It's A Blag – Volume II

Ta-Ra A Bit, Our Kid – a little book of slang used by *'Brummies'*

Reporting for Duty – West Midlands Police
(The first twenty-five years 1974 – 1999)

Top Secret Worcestershire

Top Secret Worcestershire II

The Noble Cause

Walsall's Front Line – Volume I (1997 to 1998)

Walsall's Front Line – Volume II (1998 to 1999)

By Michael Layton

Non-Fiction:

Hunting the Hooligans (With Robert Endeacott)

Tracking the Hooligans (With Alan Pacey)

Police Dog Heroes (With Bill Rogerson)

Birmingham's Front Line

Violence in the Sun

The Night the Owl Cried – A Taste of Cyprus
(With Androulla Christou-Layton)

The Hooligans are Still Among Us (With Bill Rogerson)

Proud to Serve – embracing diversity in policing

These book titles can be found on the Bostin Books Website *www.bostinbooks.co.uk* or Facebook page 'Bostin Books'.

A NOTE FROM THE AUTHORS

If you enjoyed this book, please take a moment to let others know of its existence. It will be greatly appreciated by us. Many thanks in advance!